ALCOHOLIS

Alcoholism and Codependency

ALEXANDER DE JONG

Tyndale House
Publishers, Inc.
Wheaton, Illinois

*To George G., Bob V., Izzie S., Barbara N., Ruth B., and hundreds more
in God's family who are serenely recovering, wisely detaching, and
gradually maturing one day at a time.*

Library of Congress Catalog Card Number 90-71525
ISBN 0-8423-0305-7
Copyright © 1991 by Alexander C. DeJong
All rights reserved
Printed in the United States of America

96   95   94   93   92   91
 7   6   5   4   3   2   1

*O Holy Spirit, Love of God, infuse Thy grace and descend plenti-
fully into my heart; enlighten the dark corners of this neglected
dwelling, and scatter there Thy cheerful beams; dwell in that soul
that longs to be Thy temple; water that barren soil, over-run with
weeds and briars, and lost for want of cultivating, and make it fruit-
ful with Thy dew from heaven. Oh, come, Thou refreshment of them
that languish and faint. Come, Thou Star and Guide of them that
sail in the tempestuous sea of the world, Thou only Haven of the
tossed and the shipwrecked. Come, Thou Glory and Crown of the
living, and only Safeguard of the dying. Come, Holy Spirit, in much
mercy, and make me fit to receive Thee. Amen.*

St. Augustine

What the professionals are saying about *Alcoholism and Codependency:*

"This book should be on a required reading list . . . Why? Because there is more ignorance than knowledge, more prejudice than understanding, more secrecy than openness when it comes to alcoholism and codependency than for almost any other condition afflicting the human race. Many books have been written about alcoholism. Some by recovering alcoholics who are not Christians; others by Christians who are not alcoholics. But the author of this book speaks from the inside, as both a Christian and a recovering alcoholic.

"Disaster is but a short step ahead of many drinkers. I know. I am one of those who, somewhere along the line, lost my moderation. King Alcohol became an obsession, and he took me into a life of loneliness, hopelessness, and despair.

"This book will help suffering families to understand what is happening to their loved one. It will give them guidance on how they can help, and where to go for help themselves.

"The program offered in this book can introduce you, even if you are not an alcoholic, to a new dimension of contentment and inner peace. [With this book,] you will be on your way to discovering what Paul meant when he wrote, 'I have learned that in whatsoever state I am, therewith to be content' (Philippians 4:12)."

> *Jack Hywel-Davies , Author and Broadcaster,*
> *Presenter of BBC's Radio 4 Sunday morning program,*
> Morning Has Broken

"The words of the prophet Hosea, 'My people are destroyed for lack of knowledge,' are tragically applicable today to the growing crisis within churches posed by the disease of chemical dependency and codependency. Many of God's people (both individuals and families) are being destroyed for lack of knowledge about this disease — how to recognize it, how to treat it, how to find recovery from its devastating effects.

"Alexander DeJong's book is an extraordinarily valuable gift from God for individuals and congregations concerned about this problem. With full and faithful Christian conviction and in a clear and concise style, Dr. DeJong in this one book supplies all the knowledge so desperately needed for an effective healing response. As a recovering alcoholic clergyman, and as a family therapist and a certified alcoholism counselor, and as a clinical director of an alcoholism/ drug abuse treatment program, I strongly recommend this book to anyone in the church who wants to be part of the solution to this most urgent problem."

> *Robert J. Weinhold, Associate Director,*
> *Calvary Rehabilitation Center, Phoenix, Arizona*

"Having worked for many years with families struggling with alcoholism, I have become convinced that the family members become at least as unhealthy as the alcoholic. *Everyone* in an alcoholic family is affected. *Everyone* needs help. *Everyone* needs a recovery program. Dr. DeJong's new book gives a broad outline of the problem and points families to some very valuable resources. Dr. DeJong's theological training and organizational ability are most appreciated. Concerned Christians will do well to have this book on their bookshelves."

Dr. Richard E. Grevengoed, Executive Director, Christian Care Center, Lansing, Illinois

"Dr. DeJong has done it again; more down-to-earth help, hope, and healing for alcoholics and their loved ones! Every page in this little catechism of concrete answers to complex questions is worth gold. A profoundly biblical and deeply spiritual approach to alcoholism and codependency that won't disappoint."

Prof. H. David Schuringa, Department of Practical Theology, Westminster Theological Seminary, Escondido, California

"The impression [in the church] is that Christians do not drink. This is contrary to the facts. The problem of alcohol and the Christian is present and becoming more acute. I believe Dr. DeJong is doing a genuine service in addressing this problem.

"I am impressed with the volume of valuable information contained in this book. I value Dr. DeJong as a good friend, and respect him as an outstanding scholar. I also know his deep concern for those who are involved with alcohol. I recommend this book as a source of general information about the nature and treatment of alcoholism [and codependency], and also as a sensitive attempt to address the subject in a Christian context."

W. J. Ern Baxter, Spring Valley, California,

"Dr. Alexander C. DeJong's *Alcoholism and Codependency* not only provides us with the valuable catechism that helps us understand alcoholism, but also teases apart the intricate attitudes and prevailing ambiguities regarding alcohol abuse within the Christian community. As a recovering alcoholic and a minister of the gospel, DeJong knows his subject better than he wants to. We must take the material he presents us very seriously indeed."

Joel Nederhood, The Back to God Hour / Faith 20, Palos Heights, Illinois

"Dr. DeJong's earlier book, *Help and Hope for the Alcoholic,* filled a real need for Christians and has been used widely. Now *Alcoholism and Codependency* answers many of the questions Christians ask when confronted with problems arising from the disease of alcoholism. Dr. DeJong writes from a background of personal involvement and caring. This book will be welcomed by many whose lives are affected by alcohol."

Joyce C. DeHaan, M.D., P.C., Portage, Michigan

"Dr. DeJong has chosen the important questions that Christians ask about alcoholism and codependency, and other addictive diseases. His years of experience in researching the answers to these questions, and answering them in Christian settings, allows him to give accurate and sensitive responses to difficult questions. As a Christian physician working in addiction medicine, I welcome this book for use in any setting where Christians gather looking for answers to these difficult questions."

Martin Doot, M.D., Vice President, Medical Services, Parkside Medical Services Corporation, Park Ridge, Illinois

CONTENTS

PART THREE Journey Into Recovery

PREFACE
Questions People Ask about Alcoholism

In 1982, Tyndale House Publishers released my book *Help and Hope for the Alcoholic.* Since then, I've preached in many churches, visited Christian college campuses, conducted surveys and workshops in twenty-five Christian high schools across the country, and worked with PTA organizations. Everywhere I've gone, I've encountered people who have difficult questions — questions that call for answers from a perspective that honors Christ. Some even asked their hard questions secretly, ashamed to admit that alcoholism existed in their homes, yet desperate to find the answers they needed.

Many of the questions in this book come from these hurting people. Others come from caring members of the Christian community who want more information on helping alcoholics and their families. The answers are brief; I've compiled them using materials from many points of view. Addiction counselors, Christian physicians, longtime members of AA and Al-Anon, pastors, teachers, and others have helped me. Many of these persons are mentioned by name as resources in answer to the last question (see page 125).

The answers in this book are my responsibility; they were forged in my own recovery experiences, and drawn from wide reading and open exchange with the people I met in my travels.

I have listened to questions often asked in pain, and discovered joy in the relief the questioners felt as we worked together to forge answers. And though the answers we found often were incomplete and tentative, they were a step forward on the road to healing and wholeness.

For eleven years I have walked with the Lord through recovery, and I am grateful to be able to share my experience. The path was not always easy, nor were the directions clearly marked. But Jesus' presence gave meaning to each step. In his name, then, and praying he will minister through me, I send this handbook of basic information to the congregations he loves.

One note: Throughout this book I have used the masculine pronoun *he*. This does not in any way imply that most alcoholics are male. The number of female alcoholics is increasing with alarming speed. However, the English language still has no singular personal pronoun referring to both sexes, and *he/she* tends to be cumbersome, so in this book the pronoun *he* is used to refer to a "human being."

Finally, I am especially indebted to my wife, whose patient and wise love makes recovery serene, and whose editing skills are evident in the lucid language, precise sentence construction, and readable style of this book.

Alexander C. DeJong

PART ONE

The Puzzle
of Alcoholism

ONE: Defining Alcoholism

What are some commonly accepted definitions of alcoholism? ◆ What are some facts that will help me better understand alcoholism and its effects? ◆ What causes alcoholism? ◆ Is there a brief description of alcoholism's physiology? ◆ What three factors work together in forging the chains of alcohol addiction? ◆ What is the disease concept of alcoholism? ◆ Why is alcoholism called a primary and progressive disease? ◆ Is the disease view of alcoholism widely held? ◆ Are there other views on alcoholism? ◆ Does viewing alcoholism as a disease mean alcoholics aren't responsible for their actions? ◆ How do the symptoms of alcoholism and drug addiction compare? ◆ Is alcoholism unique, in a class by itself?

TWO: Defining an Alcoholic

Who is most likely to become an alcoholic? ◆ Is the biochemical/genetic X-factor the exclusive cause of alcoholism? ◆ Is it inevitable that "genetically predisposed" persons will become alcoholic? ◆ Why is alcoholism difficult to recognize? ◆ What is the difference between drunkenness and

alcoholism? ◆ How can drunkenness be described? ◆ Why
do recovering alcoholics believe that taking one drink will
cause drunkenness? ◆ What is it about alcoholism that victimizes people? ◆ Why doesn't the alcoholic stop drinking?
◆ Does everyone experience the effects of alcohol in the
same way? ◆ What happens when an alcoholic experiences
"loss of control"?

THREE: Determining If Someone Is an Alcoholic

What are some red-flag signals pointing to alcoholism? ◆ Is
there a simple test that helps determine whether or not a person has a drinking problem? ◆ What is denial? ◆ What
major areas of the alcoholic's life are affected by his addiction? ◆ How can a person determine whether or not drinking has affected specific areas of daily living?

FOUR: Alcoholism and the Church

Why is the issue of alcohol use confusing to the church
community? ◆ What are the spiritual dimensions of the
disease? ◆ Does God care whether or not a Christian
drinks? ◆ What does the Bible say about alcohol? ◆ How
do Christians view alcoholism? ◆ Are abstinence-demand-
ing churches less vulnerable to alcoholism? ◆ Is it necessary to use grape juice rather than fermented wine in the
sacrament of the Lord's supper? ◆ What are the moral dimensions of alcoholism as sin and/or sickness? ◆ Is alcohol a gift of God? ◆ How can an individual practice
moderation? ◆ Why does alcohol use sometimes lead to
alcohol abuse? ◆ Are the reasons for drinking often more
significant than the act of drinking? ◆ Is it spiritually unhealthy to drink in order to avoid pain and to cope with
life? ◆ Is it morally wrong to avoid pain? ◆ What is the
greatest tragedy of alcoholism in the Christian community?

3

FIVE: Abstinence

When is total abstinence necessary? ◆ Can personal abstinence make a difference to others? ◆ How can personal abstinence become a bane rather than a blessing? ◆ Is personal abstinence the best parental example for children? ◆

ONE
DEFINING ALCOHOLISM

What are some commonly accepted definitions of alcoholism?

1. Alcoholism is present when there is a physical compulsion and mental obsession with alcohol.

2. Alcoholism is present when the drinking person no longer controls the intended intake. When, where, what, and how much one drinks frequently is unpredictable.

3. Alcoholism is present when someone continues to drink even though drinking may destroy a marriage, ruin a family, cause the loss of a job, or land one in jail. The cycle is pain . . . drink . . . temporary release . . . pain . . . more drinking.

What are some facts that will help me better understand alcoholism and its effects?

1. Two out of every three adults drink alcohol.

2. One out of seven drinkers becomes alcoholic.

3. Only 10 percent of the drinkers consume 50 percent of the beer, wine, and liquor in the country.

4. In the United States, the South and West have the most abstainers.

5. Forty percent of sixth graders in the U.S. have tasted wine coolers.

6. By the age of thirteen, a child will have seen 100,000 beer commercials on TV. The alcohol industry spends billions on advertising alcoholic beverages.

7. Two out of every three high school seniors have drunk alcohol within the last month. Five percent drink daily.

8. Alcohol claims approximately 100,000 lives a year, twenty-four times as many as all illegal drugs combined.

9. Alcohol is a factor in about one half of America's murders, suicides, and accidental deaths.

10. Alcohol is responsible for more deaths and societal damage than most of the psychedelic drugs that are illegal in this country.

11. Our society seems to encourage chemical use of every kind, but when such use becomes a problem, it is treated as a shameful disgrace.

12. Alcoholism and alcohol abuse cost the American society about $107 billion a year: $18 billion on premature births, $66 billion in reduced work effort, $13 billion for treatment.

What causes alcoholism?

No one knows for sure. Causes of alcoholism are hotly debated. There is, however, growing clinical evidence suggesting that alcoholics process alcohol in a manner different from nonalcoholic drinkers. There seems to be an X-factor, a built-in biochemical genetic factor, which predisposes some drinkers, and not others, to becoming alcoholic.

Consider this: in the brain tissue of deceased alcoholics, researchers have discovered a chemical called "tetra-hydro-iso-quinoline," abbreviated as "TIQ" or "THIQ." This highly addictive substance was not found in the brain tissue of deceased nonalcoholics.

In additional research conducted on rats, researchers found a strain of "teetotaling" rats, who would choose to die of thirst rather than drink water spiked with alcohol. When these non-drinking rats were injected with a dose of THIQ, they began to drink alcohol. In fact, rats injected with high doses of THIQ invariably became drunk. Similar experiments were carried on with monkeys, with the same results.

Is there a brief description of alcoholism's physiology?

As discussed previously, exactly how the built-in X-factor works is a riddle. Researchers such as Dr. C. Lieber at the

Bronx Veterans Administration Hospital, Dr. M. Schuckit at the University of California San Diego School of Medicine, and many others have conducted research on the way alcoholics and nonalcoholics process *acetaldehyde* (a toxic breakdown of alcohol) in their bodies. This research has shown that alcoholics eliminate this toxin at one-half the rate of nonalcoholics.

The April 18, 1990 issue of *JAMA, The Journal the American Medical Association,* contains an exciting report about gene discovery. Researchers reportedly have found a link between alcoholism and the presence of a receptor gene for dopamine. Dopamine is a neurotransmitter in the brain associated with pleasure-seeking behaviors. People drink alcohol because it makes them feel good. So finding a genetic relationship between pleasurable feelings and drinking alcohol gives added weight to the theory that some persons are "predisposed" to becoming alcoholics. Millions of dollars are being spent to devise a test that will indicate the presence of this genetic predisposition. Whatever the outcome of this research, it seems clear that there is a relationship between genetic makeup and certain kinds of alcoholism.

However, though research is giving us a better basis of understanding, Christian leaders, clergy, and pastoral counselors must keep in mind that no concept or theory regarding alcoholism and its effects has been proven absolutely. So we must continue to evaluate clinical evidence as research goes on. Likewise, long traditions of viewing alcoholism as willfully sinful, as something found only in the morally weak, as a condition that is readily overcome by prayer, and so forth, must be reevaluated. It is true that such trains of thought are not easily displaced or modified. But it is becoming increasingly clear that physical susceptibility combined with alcohol intake can lead to alcoholism, and to a wide variety of psychological, spiritual, and physical problems.

Of course, susceptibility to alcoholism, even if it is rooted in genetic and metabolic factors, does not absolve alcoholics from moral responsibility. But when we in the church learn to see this disease for what it is, it will help both addicts and their families find the way to wholeness and responsible decision making.

What three factors work together in forging the chains of alcohol addiction?

The three main factors in the physiology of an alcoholic that differ from the physiology of a drinker who does not become an alcoholic seem to be: (1) the time it takes the liver to break down alcohol, (2) the chemicals produced in the metabolic process, and (3) the way some of these chemicals enter the brain. (A detailed, clinically documented description of these physiological factors can be found in many books dealing with the disease concept of alcoholism.)

These technical discussions, important as they are, lie outside the scope of this brief book. However, awareness of these facts helps us understand something about the baffling disease of alcoholism. This discovery concerning the physiology of the alcoholic is not the whole answer, but it certainly demonstrates that the cause for alcoholism cannot be summarized and dismissed with the one word so many would like to use: sin.

James R. Milan and Katherine Ketcham, in their book *Under the Influence* (New York: Bantam Books, 1984), write: "While physiological, cultural, and social factors definitely influence the alcoholic's drinking patterns and behavior, they have no effect on whether or not he becomes an alcoholic in the first place. The alcoholic's enzymes, genes, and brain chemistry work together to create his abnormal and unfortunate reaction to alcohol."

Current research demonstrates that genetic predisposition toward alcoholism, plus ten to twenty years of sustained drinking — even moderate drinking — are the two most commonly identifiable factors in an alcoholic's history.

What is the disease concept of alcoholism?

First you need to know that we define a disease as "some abnormal functioning in a person with specific causes, predictable symptoms, and a prescribed course of treatment." Many believe alcoholism fits this definition. There is a good possibility of recovery or permanent remission with alcoholism if the alcoholic abstains from alcohol completely. In this view, alcoholism is considered a *primary* disease. In other words, it is not considered a symptom of some deeper psychological or social problem.

It is also considered a *chronic* disease. Recovery is possible, but relapse stalks the alcoholic all his life. Remission may be permanent if the addict works the AA program in the presence and power of Jesus Christ.

It is a *progressive* disease. Unchecked, it gets worse. Many believe total abstinence is essential for remission and recovery.

It is a *treatable* disease. (Methods of treatment will be discussed later.)

It is a 100 percent *fatal* disease, if left untreated.

Why is alcoholism called a primary and progressive disease?

When people consider alcoholism a "primary" disease, this means alcoholism is not a symptom of another problem, such as work pressure, a deteriorating marriage relationship, or a psychological disturbance. However, it is true that many symptoms that mask the primary disease can grow from the root of alcoholism.

Alcoholism is progressive. It only gets worse if left untreated. It must be noted that when alcoholism starts on a downward spiral, there may be periods of improvement when it seems that the disease is being conquered. Unfortunately, this seldom is the case. In the view of alcoholism as a disease, alcoholism is never cured; it only enters remission. So one cannot grow slack in being aware of or dealing with the disease, even in remission or during periods of sobriety. To do so will more often than not result in a reoccurrence of the problem.

Is the disease view of alcoholism widely held?

Yes. Since 1973 the American Medical Association, the American Hospital Association, the American Psychological Association, the National Association of Social Workers, the American College of Physicians, and other health organizations have *officially* pronounced alcoholism a disease.

Are there other views on alcoholism?

Yes. Some researchers disagree with the disease concept. They view alcoholism as more of a behavioral disorder, and an alcoholic as someone for whom heavy drinking has become a "central activity," or a main activity that plays a part in that person's identity, values, behavior, and choices. Those who hold this view further believe that: alcoholism does not have an overall single cause; physical, personal, and social characteristics combine to predispose a person to abuse alcohol; immediate events in a person's life trigger episodes of heavy drinking; and no single method of treatment can be effective for everyone who abuses alcohol. These researchers support "controlled drinking" rather than abstinence, and believe treatment programs must be individualized according to an alcoholic's personality, personal and environmental characteristics, drinking patterns, and motives for drinking. (Herbert Fingarette, *Heavy Drinking: The Myth of Alcoholism as a Disease*, [Berkeley: University of California Press, 1988], 100, 107, 114).

However, most recovering alcoholics today, particularly those who have undergone treatment through AA, believe that having an occasional drink is in no way an option.

Does viewing alcoholism as a disease mean alcoholics aren't responsible for their actions?

No! Look at the Twelve Steps of the AA program (page 91). Consider the action words in those twelve steps: "We admitted" (Steps 1 & 5); "came to believe" (Step 2); "made a decision to turn" (Step 3); "made a moral inventory" (Step 4); "were entirely ready" (Step 6); "humbly asked" (Step 7); "made a list" and "became willing to make amends" (Step 8); "made direct amends" (Step 9); "continued to take" (Step 10); "sought," "praying," "power to carry out" (Step 11); "to carry this message" and "to practice" (Step 12). This twelve-step program is energy packed. Recovering alcoholics work the steps — and the emphasis falls on *work.*

Don't miss the paradox. On the one hand, viewing alcoholism as a disease or illness emphasizes passivity; you can't choose to have or not have a disease. On the other hand, the illness does not control the person who gets it. So alcoholism, though it is the result of genes and metabolism, does not paralyze the alcoholic. He still holds (and demonstrates in everyday activities) the power of choice! He cannot control whether or not he becomes an alcoholic, but he can choose whether or not he stays one. Here, then, is a blend of activity-passivity that cannot be described so much as it is experienced—particularly in the pure miracle of surrender to God.

Think about Paul's words in Philippians 2:12-13: "Work with anxious concern to achieve your salvation, not only when I happen to be with you but all the more now that I am absent. It is God who, in his good will toward you, begets in you any measure of desire or achievement" (NAB). The alcoholic's actions are his, yet they also are a result of God working in his life. God's healing love can draw the alcoholic from desperation into recovery, one day at a time.

How do the symptoms of alcoholism and drug addiction compare?

Take a look at the following chart (which uses prescription drugs, but can apply to drugs in general):

Alcoholism

I. Growing preoccupation
   A. Anticipation of drinking
      1. Drinking during daytime activities
      2. Drinking during vacations (e.g., fishing trips become drinking binges)

      3. Growing involvement with drinking-related activities (e.g., building a bar, wine-making, frequenting parties where there is drinking, etc.)

II. Growing rigidity in life-style
   A. Specific times for drinking during the day
   B. Self-imposed rules begin to to change
   C. Will not tolerate interference with drinking times

   D. Limits social activities to those that include drinking

Drug Addiction

I. Growing preoccupation
   A. Anticipation of drug usage
      1. Keeping track of prescribed times for dosage
      2. Growing number of physical and emotional complaints requiring relief through drugs

II. Growing rigidity in life-style
   A. Specific times for drug usage during the day
   B. Can't go anywhere without drug supply
   C. Will not tolerate attempts to limit or change times or amounts of drug usage

Alcoholism

III. Growing tolerance
   A. "Wooden leg" syndrome—
      ability to hold large quantities
      of liquor without visible
      effects
   B. Ingenuity about drinking
      without others being aware

      1. Ordering "stiffer" drinks
         (e.g., doubles)

      2. Self-appointed bartender
         at social gatherings
      3. Sneaking drinks

      4. Drinking prior to social
         engagements

      5. Purchasing liquor in greater
         Quantities (half-gallons,
         cases)
      6. Protecting supply by
         hiding bottles at home,
         in car, at work, etc.

IV. Loss of control
   A. Increasing blackouts

   B. Unplanned drinking or
      drinking greater amounts

   C. Binge drinking

   D. Morning drinking

V. Repeated harmful consequences
   resulting from alcoholism
   A. Family
      1. Broken promises to
         "cut down" drinking
      2. Drinking during family
         activities (holidays,
         birthdays)

Drug Addiction

III. Growing tolerance
   A. Need to increase dosage
      and/or number of different
      drugs to get same benefits/
      effects
   B. Ingenuity in obtaining
      drugs without others being
      aware
      1. Seeking out a variety of
         physicians and dentists
         for prescriptions
      2. Attempting to get refill-
         able prescriptions
      3. Buying from several
         drugstores
      4. Using several drugs in
         combination for the syn-
         ergistic effect (e.g., a
         barbituate and an alco-
         holic drink)
      5. Using the drug for longer
         than called for in original
         prescription
      6. Protecting supply by
         hiding it

IV. Loss of control
   A. Increasing blackouts and
      memory distortion
   B. Larger and more frequent
      doses than prescription
      indicates
   C. Using another person's
      prescription

V. Repeated harmful consequences
   resulting from drug usage
   A. Family
      1. Frequent blackouts, which
         lead to many broken promises
      2. Inappropriate behavior
         during family activities
         (holidays, birthdays)

Alcoholism	**Drug Addiction**

Alcoholism

   3. Sacrificing family needs to purchase alcohol

   4. Physical fights or arguments about alcohol usage

   5. Threats of divorce

B. Legal

   1. Traffic violations, arrests for driving while intoxicated

   2. Drunken and disorderly conduct

   3. Lawsuits resulting from impaired judgments

   4. Divorce proceedings

C. Social

   1. Loss of friendships

   2. Hobbies, interests, community activities neglected

D. Occupational

   1. Absenteeism

   2. Lost promotions due to poor performance

   3. Threats of termination

   4. Loss of job

E. Physical

   1. Numerous hospitalizations

   2 Medical advice: "Cut down"

   3. Using alcohol as medication to relieve stress, to get to sleep

F. Growing defensiveness

   1. Vague and evasive answers

   2. Inappropriate responses to consequences of drinking

   3. Avoiding discussion of drinking

Drug Addiction

   3. Sacrificing family needs to obtain drugs

   4. Changing family duties due to physical incapacity, more time spent sleeping, lack of motivation and drive

   5. Drug-induced mood changes creating uncertainty and suspicion in family members

B. Legal

   1. Buying and/or selling illegal drugs

   2. Disorderly conduct

   3. Lawsuits resulting from impaired judgments

   4. Divorce proceedings

C. Social

   1. Loss of friendships

   2. Hobbies, interests, community activities neglected

D. Occupational

   1. Absenteeism

   2. Lost promotions due to poor performance

   3. Demotions due to impaired and inappropriate behaivor

   4. Loss of job

E. Physical

   1. Numerous hospitalizations

   2. Increasing number of emotional and physical complaints

   3. Physical deterioration due to chemical use

F. Growing defensiveness

   1. Vague and evasive answers

   2. Inappropriate responses to consequences of drug use

   3. Avoiding discussion of drug use

Is alcoholism unique, in a class by itself?

Alcoholism is, in some ways, unique. It is not at all like getting cancer or catching a cold. This complex disease possesses five intersecting and overlapping areas of "dis-ease" or malfunction. The *spiritual* (religious), the *emotional,* the *intellectual,* the *social,* and the *physical* aspects of a person's life and personality overlap and intertwine. Each area is affected, or "gets sick," in its own way. It is probably more correct to speak of "alcoholism*s*" rather than just alcoholism in general.

TWO
DEFINING AN ALCOHOLIC

Who is most likely to become an alcoholic?

This question is extremely important! Based on statistical evidence, persons belonging to certain groups are more likely to become alcoholic than others. Study this list carefully. If you belong in one or more of these categories, be doubly aware that you may well be susceptible to the disease of alcoholism.

High risk groups are:

1. *Those whose parents or grandparents were alcoholic,* or whose blood relatives have suffered from alcoholism.

2. *Those who live in big cities, particularly in low-income and poverty areas.* Poverty, low self-esteem, hopelessness, feelings of resentment, discrimination, joblessness, and apathy can create a desire to escape into alcoholism. Also, high rates of abuse in families often occur in these situations, as well as higher crime and suicide rates. These tragedies push many toward the "escape route" of alcohol and drugs.

3. *Adolescents* are a high risk because they are still in the process of maturing physically, emotionally, and spiritually. Unfortunately, emotional and spiritual growth are seriously stunted by regular or even casual alcohol use during adolescence.

4. *Those who experience severe trauma,* such as the death of a loved one, financial loss, loss of a job or position, or worries about health. People in these circumstances often use alcohol to

dull the pain of awareness. When one uses alcohol in this manner, he is placed at an even higher risk. The alcohol seems to work; nothing seems as bad after a drink or two. People often return to such a seemingly effective escape hatch.

5. *Those who are retired and elderly* often experience loneliness, empty hours, physical problems, eroding hope, boredom, apathy, rejection, and disillusionment. For many in our society, aging offers little joy. To mask pain and combat boredom, some elderly people drink alcohol, often combined with prescription drugs. Such use inevitably brings despair and alcoholism.

6. *Native Americans* have a high incidence of chemical dependency. One cause may be the pervasive hopelessness that often seems to settle over these large groups like a heavy cloud.

Is the biochemical / genetic X-factor the exclusive cause of alcoholism?

Some experts say yes. Others in the field of addiction claim that consistent abusive drinking invariably results in *psychological* dependence, even without the genetic X-factor.

Specialists in addiction disagree about the causes of alcoholism. However, there is universal agreement that the illness requires treatment without delay. Long arguments about the causes of alcoholism can be nonproductive and provide an excuse for doing nothing.

Is it inevitable that "genetically predisposed" persons will become alcoholic?

No. In light of the fact that one in ten drinkers becomes alcoholic, we must note three things:

1. Regular alcohol use — even small amounts — can trigger alcoholism.
2. Although there are exceptions, persons who use alcohol infrequently probably will not become alcoholic.
3. Ten to twenty years of moderate drinking will usually result in the genetically predisposed person crossing the line into alcoholism.

Notice well! Moderate drinking, not necessarily abusive drinking, can progress into alcoholism. Many assume that only excessive drinking causes alcoholism. This is not always true. The moderate drinker can (and often does) undergo a change in alcohol usage without realizing what is happening. Genetic pre-disposition coupled with sustained moderate drinking often results in alcoholism.

Why is alcoholism difficult to recognize?

The key word in recognizing alcoholism is "control." About 95 percent of the alcoholics in society cope well and seem to function normally. Sometimes the alcoholic is able to control his drinking; at other times his drinking is out of control. However, his life is tied to drinking. Anything can happen!

Most of the time the coping alcoholic keeps the blood level of ethanol just high enough for personal comfort. He wears a mask of well-being, sobriety, and normal spiritual life. Only those close to him know the bitterness of his bondage.

What is the difference between drunkenness and alcoholism?

These two terms often are confused, and even mistakenly considered synonymous. *Drunkenness* is self-inflicted, and follows the decision to "hang one on" or "live it up." Drunkenness often involves driving while drunk, moral dissolution, and irresponsible behavior of all kinds. A hung-over drunk is often filled with regrets.

Alcoholics act differently. Many are not often noticeably intoxicated. They may be successful at their jobs, and are not recognized as alcoholics. Others drink to find oblivion; they seek escape from a life which has become difficult or unbearable. At some point, though, willpower and freedom of choice succumb to the bondage of addiction.

Inner drivenness, compulsion, and *victimization* are key words in understanding alcoholism. To be sure, no one forces an alcoholic to take that first drink. It is his choice, generated by what is, to him, some inner power, irresistible urge, or irrational craving. When this craving becomes strong enough, the alcoholic is out of control. This means he cannot control *how much* or *when* he will drink. Sometimes he does not drink himself into intoxication; sometimes he does. Sometimes he comes straight home from work; sometimes he does not. He is no longer capable of normal decision making. Unpredictability is king; delusion reigns.

The drunkard, then, freely chooses to drink. The alcoholic is driven to drink by addictive compulsions. Though they may, on the surface, appear to be living the same life-style, they are not. There is a vast difference.

How can drunkenness be described?

Drunkenness can best be described by its signs: slurred speech, loss of motor control, inability to walk a straight line, loud one-way conversation, boisterous behavior, repetitious and offensive speech, nausea resulting in vomiting, passing out, waking up with a hangover. The list is well known. These indicators usually cluster around activities that the Bible calls "reveling, rioting, orgies, and flagrant immoralities."

Why do recovering alcoholics believe that taking one drink will cause drunkenness?

A recovering alcoholic knows his first drink will lead to drunkenness. His body reacts to alcohol differently than does the body of a nonalcoholic. For the alcoholic, one drink triggers a chemical process that leads to addictive drinking. So, for the alcoholic, one drink is too many — and a hundred drinks are not enough!

What is it about alcoholism that victimizes people?

Typically, alcoholism develops gradually, over a long period of time, without the drinker's conscious knowledge. It often is well established before its presence is apparent. So without knowing what has happened, the drinker has entered the unreal world of illusion. And illusion generates *denial.* Eventually, ignorance of the difference between alcoholism and willful drunkenness is joined with overpowering shame, which also creates a wall of denial for those who live with the alcoholic. ("This is *not* happening to him! After all, he's an elder in the church. He's on the Christian school board. He reads his Bible every day. He's done so much good for our community," etc.) Soon the cycle is in full force, often without anyone's conscious awareness!

The hidden ways of alcoholism daily paralyze both the alcoholic and those who live close to him. All of those involved somehow refuse to admit the reality of what is happening before their eyes. Denial is fostered because alcoholic behavior is not constant. There may be periods, even long periods, of sobriety. During these relatively calm times, the alcoholic and his family feel it is best to forget the episodes of abusive drinking. ("It was just a bad time. He was upset by something. Surely by now he has learned to limit his drinking to one or two drinks. It won't happen again! Thank God, that's all behind us.")

Unfortunately, it isn't behind them. Alcoholism doesn't just go away. One day, for no apparent reason, seemingly without external provocation, the alcoholic loses control. Usually, though, this happens because the alcoholic fails to accept his unique powerlessness over alcohol, the alcoholic loses control. Fragile hopes are smashed. Guilt, anger, rage, bitterness, pride, confusion, and a great deal of other damaging emotions and consequences resurface with a greater intensity than ever. And the family is in serious trouble.

Why doesn't the alcoholic stop drinking?

There is a delusion common to alcoholics: they honestly believe the reasons they feel low or depressed lie outside of their drinking. An alcoholic sees his spouse, kids, job, finances, tough luck, or whatever else as the reasons for his depression, bad luck, or deficiencies. In the alcoholic's eyes, he simply uses alcohol to deal with or get away from his problems.

The alcoholic seldom remembers that alcohol is a depressant, and therefore alcohol is much of the reason he is feeling low. It's true that drinking will pick him up for a little while, but when the alcohol wears off he'll be more depressed than ever. Also, alcohol abuse creates a series of fairy tales: "I need a drink to relax, to ease the tension, to get a good night's sleep." Recovering alcoholics know from bitter experience that, far from solving their problems, alcohol use carries more grief than comfort.

Does everyone experience the effects of alcohol in the same way?

No. Some people actually have a toxic reaction to small quantities of alcohol. After one or two drinks, they may experience nausea, flushing, dizziness, headache, or a combination of these reactions. These persons rarely are tempted to drink.

Most people, however, experience a pleasurable effect. This varies from "It's nice, now and then," to "Wow! I feel great!" For some, the euphoria generated by alcohol is so pleasant that they seek the experience regularly. This is when a person is likely to become compulsive, and then develop a psychological addiction to alcohol.

What happens when an alcoholic experiences "loss of control"?

Most of the time, an alcoholic can take one or two drinks and choose to stop. At other times, however, he drinks without control. Overpowering craving may explode within him like a bolt out of the blue. Normalcy is shattered by lunacy. The alcoholic himself has no idea why this happens to him. This erratic behavior baffles his friends and family. He stops, starts, controls, loses control, abstains for weeks, is drunk for days. In short, there is no pattern. He is at loose ends, and lives with a puzzling unpredictability.

THREE
DETERMINING IF SOMEONE IS AN ALCOHOLIC

What are some red-flag signals pointing to alcoholism?

Though checklists are in no way absolute, here are some things to watch for:

1. *High tolerance.* A person who is able to drink more than others without displaying ill effects. It is said that he holds his liquor well, that he can drink friends under the table.

2. *Mental preoccupation with liquor.* This person seems to think about little else other than his next drink. He anticipates having a drink at lunch. Having a good time means drinking alcohol. A party without alcohol is a bore, as though something essential is missing. For him, alcohol is extremely important at every social occasion.

3. *Gulping first drinks.* Alcoholics want pleasant feelings fast. Cocktails, beer, or wine are not used incidentally, as a Coke might be. Instead, alcohol is used to bring quick relaxation and euphoria. This drinker often will fortify himself with a couple of quick drinks before leaving for the dinner or party.

4. *Guilt feelings about drinking.* The person's personal standards of moderation undergo a change. He vaguely senses that his reasons for drinking have changed; his need for alcohol is too persistent for comfort. Christian sensitivities are blunted. Inner resentments fester. He thinks, "I should cut down."

5. *Blackouts.* This does not mean that the drinker has passed out. It means that the morning after drinking he has only partial recall of the events of the night before. The behavior he cannot remember may have seemed entirely normal to others at the time. The drinker, however, has experienced chemical amnesia.

6. Resenting discussions about personal alcohol use. People in the early stages of alcoholism dislike talking about how much they drink. This fear of discussion intensifies the unconscious need for denial. For them, there is no problem! Any serious discussion of drinking patterns will elicit excuses, projection, and even sarcastic humor. There is no honest evaluation of the issue.

7. Using alcohol as a tranquilizer, to relax. Alcohol becomes the preferred tool for relieving tension, anxiety, and other discomforts. It is especially useful because one needs no physician's prescription to use it, and because it works effectively on a temporary basis.

8. Improved performance while drinking. Another sign is people who seem to socialize more easily, perform job skills more readily, handle stress with less discomfort, and even be more physically coordinated while drinking. Such people most likely are already alcoholics.

9. Unpremeditated drinking. A person who stops "just to have a drink or two," and doesn't quit until he has had several more. He sometimes drinks more than he thinks he should. His drinking is different from what he would like it to be.

10. Mild withdrawal. A person who experiences such symptoms as tremors of the hands, stomach irritation, and sometimes profuse sweating.

11. Morning drinking. A person who takes a drink in the morning to relieve the symptoms of a bad hangover.

If you are in any way concerned about your drinking, or the drinking of someone you know, consider these red-flag signals very seriously. They can be effective warnings that alcoholism may be present.

Is there a simple test that helps determine whether or not a person has a drinking problem?

Yes. The following questions are used by Johns Hopkins University Hospital, Baltimore, Maryland, to determine if a patient is a problem drinker. They were developed by Dr. Robert V. Seliger.

Answer yes or no to the following questions:

1. Do you lose time from work due to drinking?
2. Is drinking making your home life unhappy?
3. Is drinking affecting your reputation?
4. Have you ever felt remorse after drinking?
5. Have you gotten into financial difficulties as a result of drinking?
6. Do you turn to inferior companions and environment when drinking?
7. Does your drinking make you careless of your family's welfare?
8. Has your ambition decreased since drinking?
9. Do you crave a drink at a definite time daily?
10. Do you want a drink the next morning?
11. Does drinking cause you to have difficulty in sleeping?
12. Has your efficiency decreased since drinking?
13. Is drinking jeopardizing your job or business?
14. Do you drink to escape worries or trouble?
15. Do you drink alone?
16. Have you ever had a complete loss of memory as a result of drinking?
17. Has your physician ever treated you for drinking?
18. Do you drink to build up your self-confidence?
19. Have you ever been to a hospital or institution because of drinking?

If you have answered yes to any *one* of the above questions, there is a possibility you may have a drinking problem.

If you have answered yes to any *two* of the questions, the odds are good that you are a problem drinker.

If you have answered yes to *three or more* of the questions, you definitely are a problem drinker.

What is denial?

Denial is the all-out effort of the alcoholic to avoid facing his problem or his pain. Denial looks like deliberate lying, but it isn't. It is vastly more complex and devious than outright untruth. Denial is actually a system of defense that the alcoholic has constructed to deal with his pain, shame, guilt, loss of self-esteem, loneliness, impotence, and the many other disastrous effects which plague his life as a result of alcohol abuse.

There are several common traits of a person who is in denial:

He *alibis:* "I didn't drink too much. I had the stomach flu. That's why I was nauseated."

He *blames:* "If I had a better spouse, [or more disciplined kids, or a more understanding boss,] I would not drink. Life's tough."

He *threatens:* "Get off my back or I'll come home even later tomorrow. Let supper hang!"

He *charms:* "Look, honey, let's get out by ourselves, have a few, and let the kids take care of themselves for once. You deserve a break."

He *brags:* "Wait till you see the sales report this month! I'm ahead of the others and will probably be getting my fourth diamond chip. Then we'll get that vacation for two in Hawaii."

He *distracts:* "Let's enroll in the Dobson series of family films at church. Maybe we can recapture some vital love for our marriage. I'm ready. Will you go with me?"

He *avoids:* "Let's not talk about it now, OK? I'll try to do better."

Denial has many faces and purposes. It buys time, silences accusers, and (most importantly) helps the alcoholic to continue drinking so he can anesthetize his deep pain. *Denial* is the most significant symptom of the alcoholic's illness.

What major areas of an alcoholic's life are affected by his addiction?

The body, mind, will, emotions, and soul are affected. Remember, each person is unique and each life is twisted in its own way. But the following areas are commonly affected areas:

1. The body: The addicted person experiences definite withdrawal symptoms. Good nutrition often is neglected. Damage to liver, heart, the vascular system, and other body organs usually occurs.

2. *The mind:* Mental preoccupation with alcohol becomes obsessive. Mental processes, dulled at first, may become permanently impaired. Such things as loss of memory (particularly recent memory), decreased attention span, and an inability to concentrate are common symptoms.

3. *The will:* Normal decision-making abilities are weakened. Uncertainty, vacillation, and lack of conviction blunt the will.

4. *The emotions:* Mood swings (going from exhilaration to depression) create an emotional roller coaster. Grandiose schemes concocted after the third or fourth refill will be seen as "dumb ideas" when considered during the gray dawn of the next day's hangover.

Then, too, the alcoholic projects his guilt onto others. He is filled with conflicting emotions: self-pity and shame; anger and remorse; resentment and regret. Families are totally baffled by the "Dr. Jekyll and Mr. Hyde" with whom they must contend. Nothing about him makes sense any longer. They cannot count on him for stability or reasonable judgment. He is irritable, unhappy, impatient, and impossible to please.

5. *The soul:* Spiritual disruptions contort religious and moral principles. An alcoholic's conscience loses sensitivity early in his drinking life. Spiritual sensitivities that once may have been sharp are blunted more and more easily. Spiritual "erosion" occurs early in the disease process, whereas physical abnormalities appear much later.

How can a person determine whether or not drinking has affected specific areas of daily living?

Drinking-related problems are not so easily observed when examining one's personal life. As an additional test, answer honestly the following questions which are grouped around specific areas.

1. *Marital:* Does your spouse think you drink too much? Does he/she even object to your drinking at all? Has your spouse ever threatened to leave you because of your drinking?

2. *Economic:* Do you sometimes drink even though you know you can't afford it? Are you using money for alcohol while other family and personal needs are neglected because you can't pay for them?

3. *Industrial:* Have you ever lost a job because of drinking? Have you ever missed work because of a hangover? Have you ever been threatened with the loss of a job because of drinking?

4. *Physical:* Has a doctor ever told you to cut down on drinking? Have you ever been hospitalized because of drinking or a complication caused by drinking?

5. *Social:* Do you prefer to associate with people who drink rather than with those who do not? Do you sometimes do things while drinking that you are ashamed of later? Has drinking become more important and time-consuming so that hobbies or interests you formerly enjoyed are now neglected?

6. *Spiritual:* Has your involvement with church life diminished? Are you withdrawing from small group prayer times? Is your devotional life of meditation withering? Do you feel God is pleased with the way you drink?

FOUR
ALCOHOLISM AND
THE CHURCH

Why is the issue of alcohol use confusing to the church community?

The entire range of drinking types and attitudes toward drinking is represented within the church. Some drink beer, wine, or a cocktail wisely. Others drink daily and heavily and call this indulgence "social drinking." Such excess is common in many Christian groups. Christian liberty has become careless license. Those who are alcoholic are seldom noticeably drunk. Many who do not drink regularly go on drinking binges for no discernible reason.

Finding a clear path through this maze is difficult. In judging this situation, some cry *sin!* Others shout *sickness!* Health experts hold contradictory opinions about the causes of alcoholism. Because serious thinking is hard work, many Christians ignore the problem, hoping it will bypass them. Others rely on the solutions offered in Bible-thumping sermons on the subject of "demon-rum."

Therefore, because there exists within the Christian community many styles of drinking as well as attitudes toward drinking, there is much confusion and uncertainty regarding alcohol use.

What are the spiritual dimensions of the disease?

People are desperate for answers and security in many different areas of their lives: social, psychological, physical, emotional, spiritual, and so on. Many are fervently seeking a spirituality that means something to them, yet are unable to find it. So there is a continual sense of emptiness, of something vital missing in their lives — an inner void leads to hopelessness. They feel powerless, unable to find workable and satisfying answers to spiritual problems. There is a lack of meaning in their lives and relationships. Their personal world seems out of control. They move from one addictive pattern to another. They need and want a spiritual identity, a personhood that rests content in God's love.

This spiritual aspect of a person is the basis of all the other aspects. It can be a unifying force that answers more and more questions in the other areas of life. When a person's issues regarding his spirituality are resolved, when the need every person feels for spiritual identity is met, the other aspects of living take on a new perspective. In the wake of inner peace, feelings of hopelessness are stilled. This only happens when a person is gifted by grace with a spiritual identity in God through Jesus Christ. Until one surrenders to Jesus Christ, the search goes on, and the person entangles himself in fruitless attempts to satisfy the hunger within through work, alcohol, drugs, sex, power, money . . . all ineffective substitutes for a personal relationship with God.

Does God care whether or not a Christian drinks?

Yes. The Bible says, "So whether you eat or drink or whatever you do, do it all for the glory of God" (1 Corinthians 10:31). Every sandwich eaten and cocktail enjoyed relates to God's rule. Everything one does is taken seriously by God. God's honor, his reputation, is wrapped up in our daily decisions about eating and drinking. Not every personal action is equally important in God's sight, but nothing is unimportant.

What does the Bible say about alcohol?

There are four words the Hebrew language uses for wine. They are transliterated as: *yayin, tirosh, asis,* and *shekar.* These words describe a fermented product with an alcoholic content of about 10 to 12 percent by volume.

The word *yayin* was used in the Old Testament to refer to wine that "gladdens the heart of man" (Psalm 104:15), wine that is used in temple services, and wine as the source of drunkenness. There are not two different types of wine, one secular and one sacred. The same wine (*yayin*) that caused rejoicing and gladness could also cause drunkenness.

Archaeologists have discovered elaborate wine vat systems in Palestine. Deuteronomy 16:13 relates how the grapes which were harvested in connection with the Feast of Booths were pressed by foot or with heavy stones in the wine vats. The treading out of the grapes was a joyous time in Israel. Isaiah 16:10 and Jeremiah 25:30 give us a glimpse of the joy and shouting that were part of the treading of grapes that occurred at harvest time.

Numerous biblical references are made to wineskins. Old Testament people knew what fermentation was all about. Wine was taken out of the lower vat as soon as the fermentation process began and was placed in jars or wineskins. A vent was left for the gases of fermentation to escape. Job 32:18-19 gives us a clue about fermentation: "For I am full of words, and the spirit within me compels me; inside I am like bottled-up wine; like new wineskins ready to burst." When the juice of the grapes began to ferment, the people didn't throw it away because it had progressed from grape juice to a product that could cause intoxication. They took jars and wineskins and filled them so the process could continue.

In some passages wine is viewed as a gift from God. Wine was simply one of those blessings from God, received along with many other blessings. Psalm 104:14-15, set in the context of praise to the Creator for all the wonderful works of his hands, includes wine: "[You] make grass grow for the cattle, and plants for man to cultivate — bringing forth food from the earth: wine that gladdens the heart of man." For all those blessings the proper response was praise and adoration to the Creator.

Wine was not viewed as intrinsically evil. One of the fondest wishes for people of faith in the Old Testament was to see

"The Day of the Lord." At that time God's will would be perfectly realized in the world. Amos wrote of this day and said:

> *"The days are coming," declares the Lord, "when the reaper will be overtaken by the plowman and the planter by the one treading grapes. New wine will drip from the mountains and flow from all the hills. I will bring back my exiled people Israel; they will rebuild the ruined cities and live in them. They will plant vineyards and drink their wine; they will make gardens and eat their fruit."*
> (Amos 9:13-14)

Wine was used in daily sacrifices. Wine (*yayin*) was offered up to God along with flour, oil, and lamb (Exodus 29:40). At the Festival of Harvest a worshiper feasted before the Lord on oxen, sheep, wine, or strong drink (Deuteronomy 14:26). The Old Testament simply does not give us a picture of wine as evil. It was part of daily life and was used in the worship of the Lord in sacrifices and on feast days.

The writer of the book of Proverbs suggests that if God's people honor him with their firstfruits, they may indeed expect their barns to be full and the wine vats to be bursting with wine (*tirosh*) (see Proverbs 3:9-10). To deny these affirmations of God's gift of wine within his good creation is simply to avoid the biblical texts on the subject.

The common New Testament Greek word for wine is transliterated *oinos*. Several references are made to wine in both the epistles of Paul and the Gospels. Paul seems to permit the medicinal use of alcohol in 1 Timothy 5:23: "Stop drinking only water, and use a little wine because of your stomach and your frequent illnesses." If we look carefully at the context it seems as though Timothy is ministering in a situation filled with many difficulties and tensions. These difficulties may well have caused some indigestion. It appears that Paul is prescribing a little wine as medication for relaxing Timothy so he could better digest his food. A central nervous system depressant, in moderation, could calm a person and facilitate digestion. Wine in moderation did not seem evil to the apostle Paul.

It would be inconceivable that Jesus would perform the miracle recorded in John 2 if there were something *intrinsically* wrong with wine. Jesus used wine. This further illustrates the fact that the Bible does not view wine as evil. Luke 7:33-34 records Jesus' enemies accusing him of being "a glutton and a drunkard." Jesus obviously must have used wine, but never abused it.

Modern medicine makes clear definitions of drunkenness. A driver of a motor vehicle is declared legally drunk if he has an alcohol blood level of .10 percent or more. No such precise definition is found in the Bible. The Old Testament links excessive use of wine or strong drink with conduct that is reprehensible and forbids the excessive use of wine. The New Testament has an explicit Greek word for drunkenness which is based on the verb root *methuo,* which means "to be intoxicated." The Bible most often speaks of drunkenness in terms of the conduct it produces. Think of Noah's drunkenness (Genesis 9:20 ff.), Lot's incest (Genesis 19:36-38), and Isaiah's denunciation of those guilty of a bribe (Isaiah 5:23).

The New Testament, like the Old, strongly condemns excess and drunkenness. The book of Romans lists drunkenness as a form of conduct totally unbecoming a child of God: "Let us behave decently, as in the daytime, not in orgies and drunkenness, not in sexual immorality and debauchery, not in dissension and jealousy" (Romans 13:13). Paul speaks of drunkenness and some of its ugly results in the book of Ephesians: "Do not get drunk on wine, which leads to debauchery. Instead, be filled with the Spirit" (Ephesians 5:18). Excessive sensuality leading to misuse of the body as the temple of the Holy Spirit easily follows from drunkenness.

Paul, in 1 Corinthians 5, calls for driving a drunkard from the fellowship of believers. There was no toleration for drunkenness in the Scriptures. The conduct associated with drunkenness compromised the integrity and witness of the Church, the bride of Christ.

The gospels record only one explicit warning from Christ regarding drunkenness. Luke 21:34 states, "Be careful, or your hearts will be weighed down with dissipation, drunkenness and the anxieties of life, and that day will close on you unexpectedly like a trap." An article in the *International Standard Bible Encyclopedia* (Grand Rapids, Michigan: Wm. B. Eerdmans Publishing Co., 1979, 880-881) asserts that the reason Christ didn't speak more about drunkenness was due to the fact that drunkenness was predominantly a problem of the wealthy. Since Jesus' ministry was carried on to a great extent with the common people and the poor, drunkenness would not have been something he encountered frequently. This article also states that the problem of drunkenness was largely confined to the rich and influential in the Old Testament. This explains warnings against rulers using wine and judges refraining from wine so that they could make just decisions.

So, as the above Scriptures show, scriptural condemnation of drunkenness is clear. There is nothing casual or superficial about the denunciation: "Nor thieves nor the greedy nor drunkards nor slanderers nor swindlers will inherit the kingdom of God" (1 Corinthians 6:10). Other passages, such as Romans 13:13, list drunkenness with other gross sins which are *willful, deliberate, and freely chosen*. This then is a key: *free choice* is a critical factor when trying to understand the difference between alcoholism and willful drunkenness.

How do Christians view alcoholism?

Some Christians call alcoholism a sin. Some church groups even make abstinence (no alcohol use) a test of membership. They demand a pledge of total abstinence. In this "alcoholism is sin" view, the alcoholic is seen as lacking self-control, one of the fruits of the Spirit. People who hold this view believe the breakdown of the alcoholic's moral discipline lies at the root of alcoholism.

Well, what about this view? Certainly, Christians agree that drunkenness is a sin. But there is a difference—a genuine and defined difference—between a drunk and an alcoholic. The difference is often stated like this: a drunkard could stop and change if he would; an alcoholic would stop and change if he could. This baffling difference is not reflected in the too simple statement that alcoholism is a sin.

Other Christians call alcoholism a disease. They may make a voluntary decision to abstain without condemning those who choose to drink occasionally, or they themselves may drink socially, without guilt. They regard an alcoholic drink as one of God's gifts to be used wisely with thanksgiving.

Are abstinence-demanding churches less vulnerable to alcoholism?

Churches that legislate abstinence have fewer drinking members. But the members who cannot meet this demand have a higher incidence of alcoholism than the drinking members of church fellowships who do not insist on abstinence. Alcohol drinking is a puzzling thing!

Is it necessary to use grape juice rather than fermented wine in the sacrament of the Lord's Supper?

Church leaders must use whatever best enhances the spirit of unity, fellowship, and health among its local membership. Recovering alcoholics in a church's membership *may* experience a real temptation to relapse at the table. Even the smell of fermented wine triggers strange reactions, especially in the early stages of recovery. In addition, there are hidden alcoholics who readily cite the use of fermented wine by churches as a validation for their continuing to drink. Churches must also respect the convictions of those who refuse to touch fermented wine.

The communion cup, whether filled with wine or grape juice, points the celebrant beyond himself to the blood shed by our Lord. The existence or nonexistence of alcohol in the cup has no relationship to the efficacy of the holy sacrament.

What are the moral dimensions of alcoholism as sin and/or sickness?

Alcoholism is a biochemically-based disease. Yet, within churches there is a persistent attempt to describe the alcoholic as morally weak and corrupt. These descriptions in terms of right/wrong, good/bad represent commonly accepted opinions which do not easily die.

Biblically, sin goes deeper than just a deliberate wrongdoing. Man has a natural bent away from God and his rule. So sin involves an alienation from God, which prevents us from trusting and surrendering to him.

In Galatians 5 and 6, the apostle Paul discusses the freedom Christians have in Jesus. We are no longer ruled by the law. Yet, we are hindered by the enemy of the flesh, which is our base nature.

Because of the flesh, we all are vulnerable to allurement, entrapment, limitations, vulnerability, weakness, and powerlessness. Our base nature wants independence from God, unlimited freedom, and power. Like self-centered children, we rebel against any limits — even those set by love. And so we reach beyond limits set by God for our welfare and become vulnerable to many entrapments.

When we live in the Spirit we harvest God's fruit of love, peace, joy, patience, self-control, gentleness, goodness, fidelity, and kindness. When we live in the flesh we harvest anger, jealousy, immorality, impurity, sensuality, drunkenness, and carousing. We're allured by works of the flesh. So we remain vulnerable because of brokenness.

It is in this context of *universal brokenness* that we can begin to understand what *appears* to be an alcoholic's willful disobedience. The concept of brokenness helps us see that the alcoholic's inappropriate conduct isn't willful — in fact, he *cannot* not drink because of his brokenness (which is a result of bad genes, strange metabolism, addicting body chemistry when ingesting alcohol, etc.) Note this carefully! He *is* morally responsible for the bad things he says and does when he drinks alcohol. He *is not* morally responsible for getting the disease of alcoholism. He is unable to drink as "normal" people drink. He plays no role in the physiological scenario of his body chemistry. This chemistry is his special brand of brokenness.

He does, however, play a responsible and crucial role in his recovery. He is not a pure victim. He must accept and confess his brokenness. He must decide to seek help! But even at this point of decision his choices are limited because his judgment is impaired.

Interveners who have learned to work sensitively with these moral distinctions can help alcoholics seek outside help. Unfortunately some alcoholics in late stage illness are unable to hear the love and concern of those who care deeply for them. Some are locked into delusion so tightly that they die in alcoholism. There is a point at which rational and moral discussions are irrelevant. The disease seems to shut down all rational and moral facility.

Even at this point God does intervene. Miracle stories are heard at AA meetings. Sovereign deliverance does take place! Praise God!

Is alcohol a gift of God?

God made everything good. Sinful folks disfigure good gifts. Medicine, such as aspirin, is good and helpful when used correctly. But when used incorrectly, it can cause serious illness and even death. The problem is not the medicine itself, but our carelessness or willfulness. The same idea can be applied to the use of alcohol. In itself, alcohol is not evil. Rather, it is amoral. Alcohol abuse resides in people, not in a bottle. The problem is not the drug, but the drug user.

Why may it be unwise and even harmful to use this gift?

Alcohol can be abused easily. Used wisely and well, it can "make glad the heart of man" (Psalm 104:15). But ignorance and carelessness easily lead to addiction. Earlier we mentioned genetic predispositions, heredity factors, and other red-flag signals which call out for serious attention. To forget this is folly!

No one ever uses or abuses in isolation. We are members of God's worldwide family. Interpersonal relationships functioning with honesty, openness, understanding, and love make us happy. Healthy togetherness creates self-esteem and maximizes God-created potential. Alcohol destroys this delicate web of togetherness. Broken promises, rash words, surly isolation, betrayed love, raw carelessness, and a lot more are the daily diet of many hidden alcoholic families.

How can an individual practice moderation?

A person who drinks must realize how even small amounts of alcohol can impair behavior. Intoxication depends on several factors, including age, body weight, amount of food eaten, sex, fatigue, amount of alcohol in drinks, and mental state. The following information about alcohol can help to establish limits: One twelve-ounce beer equals one four-ounce glass of wine equals one ounce of hard liquor. A drinker must determine how much alcohol he can drink safely within one hour without becoming intoxicated. It is important to remember that the same individual can react differently to the same chemical at a different time, and that a mood change can change a reaction to any chemical. Carelessness is a sure way to immoderate use.

Why does alcohol use sometimes lead to alcohol abuse?

Every drink of wine, beer, or hard liquor involves using a drug. Too many Christians enjoying Christian freedom forget this simple but awesome fact! Alcoholic drinks contain ethanol, which affects the outer layer of the brain. It easily fogs self-awareness. It may desensitize the decision-making control centers of the brain. It may lower the perception of moral standards. This drug is no different from prescription drugs — it can be beneficial, but only if used properly! It must never be used casually, naively, carelessly, or ignorantly.

Drinking a beer or two may be morally permissible, but it easily becomes selfish indulgence. Careless regard of a recovering person who is present is violating neighborly love. And paying no attention to how much one drinks can easily lead to legal drunkenness. Forgetting that adults are role models for young Christians displeases our Lord.

When deciding whether or not to drink, consider Paul's words:

> *I freely admit that all food is, in itself, harmless, but it can be harmful to the man who eats it with a guilty conscience. We should be willing to be both vegetarians and teetotallers if by doing otherwise we should impede a brother's progress in the faith. Your personal convictions*

*are a matter of faith between yourself and God, and you
are happy if you have no qualms about what you allow
yourself to eat. Yet if a man eats meat with an uneasy
conscience about it, you may be sure he is wrong to do so.
For his action does not spring from his faith, and when we
act apart from our faith we sin.* (Romans 14:20-23, *Phillips*)

Are the reasons for drinking often more significant than the act of drinking?

People use alcohol because it makes them feel good. It is the
reasons one has for wanting to feel good that need honest examination. Christians know that an unexamined life is a substan-
dard and stunted life.

Many factors are involved in drinking. Some people, adults
as well as adolescents, drink because of peer pressure. Others
drink because it gives them a sense of adventure. Some drink to
make a statement; a defiant protest against church, school, or
parental authority. Still others drink only when a perceived
crisis occurs, to unwind and to relieve pain and stress.

Examining one's reasons for drinking is necessary because a
moderate drinker can be an early stage alcoholic without seem-
ing to exhibit any signs of alcohol abuse. Unconsciously and
subtly, drinking begins to perform certain "helpful" functions in
the moderate drinker's life. It helps him cope; provides escape
from bad feelings like fear, low self-esteem, anger, or inferior-
ity; becomes a "friend" that seems to banish loneliness and
isolation; lifts one into a fantasy world, out of what often is a
harsh reality. All of these "helping" functions are "red-flag"
warnings that the drinking is on its way to being out of control.
(A helpful tool to use in examining reasons for drinking is the
set of "Feeling Charts" in Vernon Johnson's excellent book
I'll Quit Tomorrow [New York: Harper and Row, 1980], 9).

Remember this: Anyone using alcohol to alter moods and
change perceptions cannot relate honestly or openly with other
people. Love is the fundamental standard for every action,
drinking included. Whenever you choose to drink, ask yourself
why you are drinking. Your reason is often much more important than the act itself.

Is it spiritually unhealthy to drink in order to avoid pain and to cope with life?

Pain relief is always temporary. One can never be totally free from pain. The false euphoria of alcohol/drug relief obscures the causes of pain, which seems beneficial to the user. Unfortunately, this method of pain relief only prevents one from resolving the issues that need to be resolved, which results in stunted spiritual development and relationships. To be spiritually and emotionally healthy, one must face the issues in his or her life, using *all* experiences — even painful ones — to grow into wholeness.

Is it morally wrong to avoid pain?

In and of themselves, pain and relief are neither moral nor immoral. Life is tough and involves all kinds of suffering. As stated previously, pain helps one grow, but no one — not even Christians — should ever endure pain for pain's sake. God works in all things, pain included, for good. God also provides comfort and healing through his Spirit and his Word. He also has given us the intelligence and abilities to develop drugs that can help provide comfort and healing when used correctly, under the supervision of a physician.

What is the greatest tragedy of alcoholism in the Christian community?

The greatest tragedies are not reported in newspapers. There are obviously tragic reports of drunken drivers, innocent children slaughtered, and youthful suicides. But these tragedies are not what cause pain to the greatest numbers of people. In thousands of Christian families, the disease of alcoholism lurks unobserved or denied. Its accompanying problems — sexual and physical abuse of spouses and children, violent language, sullen silences, broken promises, misguided prayer requests, and a lot more — scar many lives. Wives and husbands hang on to marriage in self-pity and self-imposed martyrdom while friends praise them as heroes for toughing it out. Sincere worshipers desperately hope for a miracle of deliverance without knowing exactly what they want or need.

FIVE
ABSTINENCE

When is total abstinence necessary?
   1. When one is chemically dependent or alcoholic.
   2. When one is taking certain prescribed medications.
   3. While one is operating equipment such as an automobile, a lawn mower, power tools of any sort, a boat, etc.
   4. While one is engaged in athletics.
   5. During pregnancy.
   6. Whenever full cognitive functioning is required, such as in the classroom, on the job, during a performance.

Can personal abstinence make a difference to others?
   Choosing not to drink will not prevent someone else from abusing alcohol or becoming alcoholic. Personal actions do not control another's actions. Genetic structure, metabolism, and body chemistry produce alcoholism. Willful abusers are self-driven and do what they please.
   Abstinence, however, reduces the pressure on others to drink. Peer pressure can be powerful. Many people, including some Christians, often have a drink before dinner. If someone in the party declines a drink, he may be assaulted by jocular jibes: "What's the matter? You an alchy, too? Come on, you're not against a drink, are you? Hey, the preacher's not around. Besides, he likes his booze, too!" It can be embarrassing, often

lonely, to choose not to drink. But your quiet, strong stand of abstinence may encourage someone who knows he has trouble with alcohol.

Thank God for the uncomplicated Christian who quietly chooses not to drink. He doesn't need a drink to make the occasion. Nor does he get on a soapbox to take a stand. He merely says, "No, thanks. I'll just have a glass of 7-Up."

How can personal abstinence become a bane rather than a blessing?

Making abstinence a Christian law can easily make for spiritual pride. Subtly, the abstainer can make the moderate drinker feel guilty. Abstainers unconsciously may exude a spirit of condescension, self-righteousness, and judgment. This spirit, usually not perceived by the person radiating it, often drives problem drinkers into deeper isolation.

Some Christians make abstinence a test for church membership. These rules often slam the door of healing love. Legalism, whatever its form, is bondage. Religious chains are still chains.

Is personal abstinence the best parental example for children?

It all depends. The atmosphere of the abstinent home is more important than the act of refraining from drinking. Negative remarks about friends who drink easily poison the atmosphere of the nondrinking home. It goes like this:

"We don't drink like George. We think it's more Christian not to drink. We're not saying George always drinks too much. But we don't want our kids to become drinkers like George."

Such comments foster false pride, increase guilt levels of ambivalent teenagers, intensify internal conflict in growing children, and most sadly, cut off open communication between parents and children.

Abstinence is no big deal! The abstainer feels his choice is the best choice for him. Period. Not an exclamation point. Kids easily sense the spirit of free and joyful choice.

PART TWO

Alcoholism:
A Family Disease

ONE: Alcoholism — A Complicated Problem

Why are the problems that accompany alcoholism so difficult to handle? ◆ How does the alcoholic use anger as a
weapon? ◆ How does the alcoholic use anxiety? ◆ How
does the coping alcoholic in denial complicate the puzzle?

TWO: Alcoholism and Families

Why are many families vulnerable to the ravages of alcohol abuse? ◆ How much time usually elapses before the
alcoholic's family admits to having a problem? ◆ Why is
alcoholism called a shame-based disease? ◆ How do "I
can't help it" and "You can quit" relate to each other in an
alcoholic's life? ◆ Is it an act of disloyalty to discuss the
alcoholism of a loved one with someone else?

THREE: Alcoholism and Children

What is the effect of alcoholism in the family on its young
children? ◆ How do children cope when they must live in
alcoholic homes? ◆ What are the effects of alcoholism on
adult children of alcoholics? ◆ Why do some adolescents
abuse alcohol? ◆ Why do some young people become alcoholics? ◆ Why are young people so vulnerable to alcohol

and its negative effects? ◆ Are there reliable statistics about
adolescent usage of alcohol in Christian schools? ◆ What
can parents do to help growing children avoid alcohol
abuse? ◆ Why are parents so often ineffective in preventing
adolescent alcohol abuse? ◆ What warning signs point to
adolescent alcohol abuse? ◆ What must parents do when
suspecting problem drinking? ◆ Which family practices
help prevent drinking problems?

FOUR: Codependency

What is a codependent or coalcoholic? ◆ What are some
typical reactions in a codependent family? ◆ What are some
feelings common to codependents or coalcoholics? ◆ Is the
codependent responsible for the alcoholic's sickness? ◆ Is it
prudent for a codependent to drink with an alcoholic who is
still in denial? ◆ Why do codependents need outside help?
◆ How can objective, concerned Christians help and support codependents? ◆ What are the certain fundamentals
codependents must learn in order to recover? ◆ What is an
enabler? ◆ Is enabling love all bad? ◆ Doesn't Christian
love require one to help? ◆ How can one stop enabling?
◆ What is detachment? ◆ Why must the enabler learn detachment? ◆ What kinds of persons experience the most
difficulty learning detachment?

FIVE: Intervention

What is intervention? ◆ Is intervention primarily a moral
confrontation? ◆ Who performs the intervention? ◆ What is
meant by the term, "significant other"? ◆ How do interveners integrate moral issues into their work? ◆ What specific
preparations are made by the intervention team? ◆ What
takes place during an intervention? ◆ What is meant by the
phrase "hitting bottom"? ◆ What is the difference between

honest judgment and judgmentalism? ◆ How did Jesus
avoid judgmentalism? ◆ What is the best location for an intervention? ◆ What is the place of prayer at an intervention?
◆ How does the intervention end? ◆ How can the Christian
community help facilitate intervention? ◆ What is a Family
Outreach Team? ◆ Are there Bible passages to help interveners?

SIX: The Church's Involvement

Are there many families with alcohol problems in the
church community? ◆ What positive suggestions are there
to help codependents? ◆ What are some negative things to
avoid? ◆ How can pastors, elders, and other church leaders
be equipped to deal with alcoholism in their churches and
beyond? ◆ What if the alcoholic refuses help? ◆ Should
persistently willful alcoholics in denial be removed from
church membership?

ONE
ALCOHOLISM – A
COMPLICATED PROBLEM

Why are the problems that accompany alcoholism so difficult to handle?

Alcoholism reaches deep into subconscious areas of the self. This is uncharted territory. Well-meaning people can't fix the alcoholic situation.

Dr. J. Kellerman points to this when he compares recovery from alcoholism to a Gothic arch. He says,

> *"There are unseen foundations; many persons may lay various stones in the arch; but the keystone must be put in place by the alcoholic, or the structure falls. No one can do for the alcoholic what must be done by the alcoholic. You cannot take the patient's medicine and expect the patient to benefit. Choices must be made and action taken by the alcoholic of his own volition if recovery is to occur on a permanent basis."* (J. L. Kellerman, Alcoholism: A Guide for Clergy, New York: National Council on Alcoholism, 1958).

How does the alcoholic use anger as a weapon?

He cleverly arouses others' anger and provokes loss of temper to disarm the possible helper. Flaring tempers and angry spirits prevent healing, squelch good will, and keep those who might help at arm's length. The alcoholic uses the anger of others as a justification for his own drinking.

The proverb, "The gods make angry those whom they wish to destroy," has a valid point. Angry alcoholics destroy loved ones, at least for the moment. Alcoholics are addicts who will use any excuse to keep on drinking. Their mental world is a strange place, manufacturing demons of projection and illusion.

How does the alcoholic use anxiety?

He uses anxiety in others to manipulate them. He wants loved ones to become "codependent" by covering up for him. None involved wish to be embarrassed by a bad check, by an obscene conversation, or by any alcoholic blunder. By creating anxiety for the outcome of many situations the alcoholic has his cake (he delays paying the price for his conduct), and he eats it too (he keeps on drinking).

How does the coping alcoholic in denial complicate the puzzle?

A "coping alcoholic," for the most part, acts normally. He seldom screams, beats his spouse, or is absent from work. This is where denial comes in. Because the alcoholic can function on a more or less normal level, he doesn't believe he has a problem. Drinking is just a part of life, a way of relaxing or of rewarding himself. To the person who doesn't live close to the alcoholic, everything seems to be all right. What outsiders do not see are the mood swings, forgotten birthdays, tense holidays, sullen silences, long naps in front of the TV, joyless sex, ignored children, irrational criticism, vanishing family devotions, and much more.

TWO
ALCOHOLISM AND FAMILIES

Why are many families vulnerable to the ravages of alcohol abuse?

Today's world has brought confusing changes to traditional family life. Everything that once was held together seems to be coming unglued! The certainties that once defined meaning in daily living seem to be disappearing, slipping away. Life seems out of control to many people. The government, the educational system, law enforcement agencies, economic programs, religious denominations, and even moral systems seem unmanageable and out of reach.

The extended family is largely gone. For most people, there are very few uncles or aunts or cousins who live close enough to know and care about them or their problems. Mobility, affluence, and suburbia have taken a huge toll.

The purveyors of modern advertising messages are sowing values that shape behavior. Cleverly created desires are presented as needs that must have immediate satisfaction. In this kind of world alcohol is the great seducer. People feeling intimidated, isolated, lost, unloved, disconnected, and disoriented reach for a quick fix. And alcohol works! But merely for the moment.

Using alcohol in order to cope with life creates alcoholism in 1 out of 10 users. The drinkers who do not become alcoholic are deceived by alcohol's short-term, illusory relief. Alcohol stunts a person's growth into maturity where both pain and pleasure are accepted as part of God's good purpose for our lives.

Fragile families need to know that using alcohol can tear the tender fabric of love, respect, and dignity. Families in trouble with alcohol need knowledge, compassion, and concrete help. The answers to questions in this section are designed to help families troubled by alcohol-related problems.

How much time usually elapses before the alcoholic's family admits to having a problem?

Families ordinarily do not admit to alcoholism's presence until the illness has been critical for about seven years. After that, members often wait two more years before seeking professional help.

Why is alcoholism called a shame-based disease?

Alcoholics and their families are powerless over alcohol and suffer from unmanageability. Betrayal of confidences, broken promises, and frustrated dreams lead to shame. People close to the alcoholic view themselves as equally dependent, weak, flawed, limited, and basically deficient as the sick person.

Shame and guilt are closely related. Guilt focuses on action. One feels guilty because he cheats or lies. Shame focuses on personhood. It arises out of feelings of unworthiness, failure, or being no good.

Think of a football field. Going out of bounds makes one guilty. Failure to reach the goal makes one feel ashamed. Guilt comes when we transgress boundaries; shame arises from failure to reach a goal.

The alcoholic lies, brags, manipulates, verbally lacerates, wastes time, robs his employer, breaks promises, and much more. He feels terribly guilty, even though he loudly proclaims innocence. This is part of alcoholic insanity! The alcoholic carries a huge load of guilt, heavier and larger than most people realize. Codependents also carry a load of guilt for their irrational screams, their failure to be strong, their inability to pray, and above all for being unable to control the inappropriate drinking conduct of loved ones.

Everyone in this situation honestly wants forgiveness. They do not intentionally fail the Lord, hurt others, or let themselves down. Often, they confess their sins to Jesus, but do not feel forgiven. They think their prayers are not heard.

Shame is the swamp underneath the alcoholic's guilt. It is deeper than feeling worthy of punishment and rejection. The active alcoholic is radically out of sync. He feels victimized by metabolic processes and bad genes, and still he believes he isn't a mere victim. He's at fault. Self-esteem is gone. Desperately trying to rescue self-worth, he claims he can quit anytime. Shame paralyzes him, then leads to hopelessness and even suicide. This is especially true for the Christian who honestly wrestles with the sin-sickness dynamics of alcoholism.

The same swamp of shame mires down families who deny the existence of a problem, toughing it out by assuming all kinds of new roles in daily living, and by assuming they are failures because they can't "fix" the drinking problem at home. Shame is the poisoned atmosphere for everyone living with an alcoholic or an alcohol abuser.

How do "I can't help it" and "You can quit" relate to each other in an alcoholic's life?

Consider the following diagram:

ALCOHOLISM

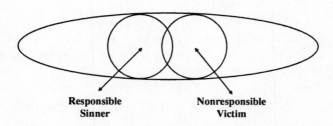

Responsible   Nonresponsible
Sinner   Victim

The elongated oval represents the alcoholism. Inside the oval are two circles, each revolving around its own center. The center of the left circle represents a "responsible sinner," the center of the right circle denotes a "nonresponsible victim." The left circle shows a person who is responsible for his thoughts, feelings, desires, and decisions. The right circle show a person who is not responsible for those things, who is a victim of his disease.

Each circle is rotating. In the process there is a point where they intersect and move within each other, meshing in such a complex and blurred way that it becomes impossible to draw clear lines at the points where the nonresponsible victim becomes a responsible sinner, or vice versa. And so the alcoholic becomes, and often remains, a unique and impenetrable combination of freedom and bondage. Yes, he is responsible — and yet he is also caught in a vicious cycle from which he seemingly cannot escape.

The alcoholic must discover victory in Jesus Christ. It is each alcoholic's personal responsibility to seek this victory, for it is only through Christ that anyone can find hope for total redemption from the terror of alcoholism.

But many alcoholics who are Christians remain caught in the snare of their illness. They (and often the Christian community around them) feel that their sickness is sin. They become overwhelmed by guilt and feel isolated, ashamed, fearful, and abandoned. Often fellow Christians know nothing of the alcoholic's anguish. So it is only through open and insightful conversation on this complicated issue that we will be able to help many Christians who are alcoholics to come out from behind the painful security of concealment and hurt.

Is it an act of disloyalty to discuss the alcoholism of a loved one with someone else?

No! It is not disloyal to alert your physician to a medical problem of a family member. Alcoholism is an illness. Open and honest discussion is not tale-bearing. It is a way of showing solicitous love.

Honest confrontation from an objective and caring Christian may produce explosive anger from the alcoholic who wishes to avoid facing his addiction at all costs. Nevertheless, strong detached love means being willing to be exposed to such anger.

THREE
ALCOHOLISM AND CHILDREN

**What is the effect of alcoholism in the family on its
young children?**

To comprehend its effect, one must realize that the nuclear
family made up of mother, father, and siblings is the only shell
of security for most children today. Because of the mobility
of our society, extended families consisting of grandparents,
assorted uncles, aunts, and cousins do not exist. Therefore, children must rely on the security, stability, and loving authority
provided by mothers and fathers. If one or both parents are
alcoholic, serious problems arise for the children. They cannot
count on their families to shield them against the stresses of life.

A child in an alcoholic family will experience *loneliness,
bewilderment,* and *rejection.*

Consider Carl, a fourth grader, who arrives home from
school to find his mother passed out on the couch. Dinner has
not been started, the home is unkept, clean clothing has not
been provided. Carl's needs for his mother's concern and ap-
proval are not met. His mother is asleep, and he doesn't really
know why. A lonely boy makes himself a peanut butter sandwich and watches TV until bedtime.

A child in an alcoholic family will experience *hurt, loss of
self-esteem,* and *rebellion* at the injustice of the situation.

Jack's dad has promised an outing of supper and basketball
for him and two friends. Arriving home raring to go, they are

met by Jack's mother who explains that Dad is sick in bed. The evening's plans are scrapped. Jack knows his dad is drunk. He loses face with his friends and becomes skeptical of what anyone who is in authority says or does.

A child in an alcoholic family will experience *fear, disillusionment, insecurity,* and *anger.*

Consider Cynthia, who upon returning home from school is greeted by a drinking father. His mood has passed from exhilaration to irrational irritation. She presents her school work to him just as he requested yesterday.

Noting the grade of "C," the dad explodes. "Is this the best you can do?" he yells. "I did better than that when I was half your age! Go to your room and rewrite this mess. Let me see it when you're through!"

The child, sobbing, goes to her room, copies the paper neatly, and presents the product to her dad, who by this time is snoring loudly on the couch, unable to evaluate the work.

How do children cope when they must live in alcoholic homes?

Coping mechanisms vary. Some exist and survive by assuming certain roles in the family. Sharon Wegscheider, in her book *Another Chance* (Palo Alto: Science and Behavior Books, 1981), has identified the following roles adopted by children in alcoholic families:

There is the *hero.* He is usually the oldest child. Driven by his burning desire to "fix" his family, to make it "normal" like others, he feels only failure, guilt, and inadequacy because nothing he does seems to work. But he keeps trying. In many cases he becomes an overachiever, receives some positive attention, has some feelings of self-worth, but becomes compulsive and driven in his efforts to repair, mend, and take on the world.

Another role for children in alcoholic families is that of the *scapegoat.* This child has been bruised so often by the alcoholic that he directs his life outside of the family. Carrying the hurt and blame on his shoulders, he turns to delinquency, thrives on negative attention, and may himself be destroyed by addiction.

Another child may become the *lost* child. Retreating from the ugliness of the family situation, this one seeks relief in escape, social isolation, retreat. This child is shy, lonely, and afraid.

Finally, a child who is afraid of the chaos around him may seek attention by becoming the *family mascot,* the *class clown.* He is frequently hyperactive, always on stage, ready to perform. He seeks fun above all. But the price often is prolonged immaturity and even emotional illness.

These roles, unconsciously assumed, may be switched. They may be dropped. These behaviors should be recognized as the ways in which children will try to cope with the problem of alcoholism in their homes. In various ways, children carry these roles into adulthood and so create psychological problems of all kinds. Thus, adult children of alcoholics display the tragic consequences of early life in an alcoholic home.

What are the effects of alcoholism on adult children of alcoholics?

1. They become socially isolated and especially fearful of authority figures.
2. They become approval-seekers and are frightened, intimidated, or angered by angry people and personal criticism.
3. They grow up with an over-developed sense of responsibility.
4. They harbor exaggerated guilt feelings while they assert their own rights instead of giving in to others.
5. They have lost the ability to express feelings of joy and happiness because they have learned to suppress their feelings in the presence of an addicted parent.
6. They have a very low sense of self-esteem. The atmosphere of shame in an alcoholic household results in the growing child's perceiving himself as defective and of little worth.

Why do some adolescents abuse alcohol?

Initially, young people become involved in the use of alcohol for a variety of reasons. These are peer pressure, curiosity, boredom, and rebellion against adult-imposed rules. Most adolescents, however, are just like adults; they drink because it makes them feel good! When drinking becomes habitual, teenagers cite a number of other reasons:

"All my friends do."

"It makes me feel important."

"If you had my parents, you would, too."

"I need it to unwind, to get away from school things."

"A party is not a party without booze."

"My parents do — why can't I?"

The rock-bottom truth is that people of all ages drink a lot because they want to feel good. Most other reasons are just excuses.

Why do some young people become alcoholics?

Inherited genetic predisposition plus early experimentation and regular use combines with:

1. *Low self-image:* Some young people feel unimportant or worthless. They use alcohol to feel better about themselves.

2. *Poor family support:* Well-intentioned parents, whether married, separated, or divorced, do not always agree on the rules for their children. These disagreements make children feel lost and angry. Parents also may ignore the emotional needs of their children as they mature. Young people need consistent rules with appropriate sanctions, as well as love during their teen years.

3. *Weak friendship skills:* Knowing how to make friends means reaching out to others, taking the risk of being rejected, and learning how to select positive relationships. The need to belong is a universal need, especially important to young people. Alcohol use is often viewed as a way to belong.

4. *Poor decision-making skills:* Learning how to evaluate right and wrong behavior is a complicated process. Adolescents experience both peer and parent pressure. Some find this balancing process overwhelming and may try to find an escape.

5. *Inability to express feelings appropriately:* Suppressing or not expressing feelings, being revengeful when one is angry, not forgiving others, acting tough when one is afraid and are ways of coping with feelings that result from low self-esteem. Alcohol use can temporarily mask those unpleasant feelings.

6. *A lack of purpose:* Who am I? What should I do with my life? What gives life meaning? For some it is easier to medicate the hard questions rather than to find answers. Most young people struggling with these situations do not turn to alcohol. But some do.

Why are young people so vulnerable to alcohol and its negative effects?

1. Adolescents forget that alcohol is a drug and naively assume that only older people become alcoholic. They willfully blind themselves to the fact that teenage alcoholism is on a fast-rising curve.

2. They are still growing. Even though organ damage may not be obvious, they do not grow emotionally while they use alcohol regularly. Physical growth may be normal, but emotional growth is stunted.

3. Youthful exuberance makes them vulnerable to wrong decisions resulting in mistakes with lifelong effects, such as teen pregnancy, early-stage alcoholism, dropping out of school, drunk driving catastrophe, etc.

Are there reliable statistics about adolescent usage of alcohol in Christian schools?

During a period of five years I visited twenty-seven private Christian high schools, nationwide and in Canada, consulting with faculty members and administering questionnaires to anonymous student volunteers. The schools I surveyed served both rural and urban populations, and automatically fell into three nearly equal numerical groupings of low, middle, and high use/abuse. My findings stress the urgent need for developing programs of alcohol education.

In low use/abuse schools, there were virtually no girls who

used alcohol or drugs. Usage began late, in the tenth, eleventh, or twelfth grades. Fewer than 5 percent of the seniors got drunk weekly. About 10 to 15 percent of the juniors and seniors had problems in their lives because of alcohol abuse. There was little alcohol use/abuse among fathers, and almost none among mothers. These schools were largely rural in location.

In middle use/abuse schools, the rates went up. Five to 8 percent of the seniors got drunk weekly or more. Initial alcohol use occurred in the ninth and tenth grades. Girls drank about half as often as boys. About 15 to 25 percent of the students at junior and senior levels were experiencing problems because of abusive drinking (trouble with parents, school authorities, police, church leaders, and even peers). Parental drinking was greater than in low schools, especially for the fathers.

In high use/abuse schools, the level for senior boys was as high or higher than in public schools. Ten to 20 percent of the seniors got drunk weekly or more. Girls drank at about the same rate as boys. Twenty to 40 percent of the students drank abusively (in a way which interfered with normal life functioning). There was a high level of experimentation with other drugs, notably marijuana and cocaine. Parents of these students drank much more than parents in the other two groups, and usually were more affluent and educated. In these schools, the students were more open about their drinking life-styles.

Comparing public school statistics with those of Christian schools, note the following:

1. Public school students experimented with alcohol earlier.

2. Girls in public school had a higher rate of alcohol use than girls in Christian schools.

3. The drinking patterns of seniors in both public and Christian high schools were virtually identical.

4. In college, public school graduates stopped problem drinking sooner than Christian school graduates. (Problem drinkers are those whose drinking causes conflicts with parents, teachers, police, and peers. They are not considered alcoholic.)

In PTA workshops on alcohol abuse, which were conducted in these schools, it was universally true that all the parents underestimated the problem drinking of their children and the urgent need for consistent alcohol education efforts.

What can parents do to help growing children avoid alcohol abuse?

The following guidelines have proven effective:

1. Examine personal alcohol use. Personal values and attitudes toward alcohol affect children.
2. Get accurate information about alcohol. Learn as much as you can before your children ask.
3. Learn the signs of a developing problem. Alcohol and drug problems usually develop over time, but there are definite warning signals.
4. Keep communication lines open. Don't moralize or lecture. Mutual interchange of information, not parental dictums of authority, help maturing children.
5. Work with others. Consult and cooperate with church members, community organizations, and local school boards to sponsor education and prevention programs for parents and young people. Joining support groups and encouraging healthy life-styles are good ways to learn how to live chemically free.

Why are parents so often ineffective in preventing adolescent alcohol abuse?

1. Adolescents are in the process of cutting ties with parents emotionally and socially. Peer groups assume larger roles and greater significance.
2. Parents in a mobile society are often away on mini-vacations and long weekends. They simply do not know what their unsupervised children are doing. Many drinking parties occur when parents are absent.
3. Some minimize the significance of children's drinking episodes, assuming that the young are merely passing through a temporary phase of experimentation and occasional excess, just sowing "wild oats."
4. Parents as well as children are infected by the morally permissive spirit of the present time.

5. Parents are fearful that their children will be alienated from peers if a strong stand against drinking is enforced.
6. Shame and fear prevent parents from sharing the painful experiences of discovering alcohol abuse and addiction in the family. It is sad and true that free and honest sharing in the Church is never easy!

What warning signs point to adolescent alcohol abuse?
1. A slow or sudden drop in grades.
2. A switch in friends.
3. Emotional mood swings.
4. Increasing defiance of family rules.
5. Secretive behavior.
6. Loss of initiative.
7. Withdrawal from family functions.
8. Change in physical hygiene.
9. Trouble at school.
10. Problems with the police.
11. Edginess and defensiveness.

What must parents do when suspecting problem drinking?
1. Confront the issue calmly, knowledgeably, and immediately.
2. Refuse to minimize or deny the problem.
3. Treat the behavior, and set clear standards.
4. Set standards without fear of alienating children.
5. For the time being, don't ask why or moralize.
6. Ask for help from available, confidential resources.

Which family practices help prevent drinking problems?
1. Parents modeling consistent moderation without radiating spiritually elitist attitudes.
2. Standards for using alcohol are clear, well established, and agreed upon by all.
3. Excessive drinking and drunkenness are not tolerated; they are not viewed as comical, merely a passing phase of behavior, or occasionally acceptable.

4. Drinking is viewed as morally neutral.
5. Abstinent families do not make negative remarks about others in the community who choose to drink.
6. No pressures are placed on family members or guests to drink or not to drink.

FOUR
CODEPENDENCY

What is a codependent or coalcoholic?

This is a person living close to the alcoholic. Closeness exists particularly in a family, and often to a lesser degree in a church, a school, a workplace, or in any small group. The codependent begins to show symptoms of *disease* similar to those of the alcoholic. The codependent is not chemically sick, but reacts to his contact with alcoholism in unhealthy ways.

Nonalcoholic persons dislike being called coalcoholics. They even resist being called codependents. Denial is as real for them as it is for the alcoholic.

What are some typical reactions in a codependent family?

1. Family members *deny* the existence of a problem. They cover up for the alcoholic and for each other. "Our family is OK!"

2. *Word battles* are common. Coalcoholics reason, plead, threaten, cajole, promise, demand, and lecture. Behavior changes occur. Well-meaning "helpers" avoid possible embarrassing social situations, refuse to buy liquor, hide supplies in the house, measure bottle levels, cover up, etc. Codependents try to control the drinking patterns of the alcoholic. These efforts are bound to fail since codependents can't cure the disease! In their frustration, they lose self-esteem, become insecure, depressed, and even blame themselves for the sick person's drinking.

3. The family becomes *disorganized*. A what's-the-use spirit smothers members with paralysis, anger, fear, and guilt. Children feel rejected in this confusion. Many codependents assume they are "turning the other cheek," or "going the second mile," as they continue to cope with the erratic behavior of the alcoholic. They do not seek help, but continue to slog along in gray despair.

4. Families *reorganize*. Members assume unnatural roles. A sober spouse assumes roles once held by the alcoholic. Children become heroes, mascots, wimps, rebels, or just plain lost.

5. Family *separations* occur. A spouse leaves. Young adults exit from the family home to live elsewhere. If a spouse cannot live apart for financial or other reasons, he or she will leave emotionally. This inner retreat makes for resentments, emotional numbness, and fearful loneliness.

6. *Alcoholism lies hidden* under layers of ignorance, denial, shame, guilt, and failure. As a result, when such separations occur, families fail to alert helping pastors to the underlying cause of discord.

7. The *scars* of codependency are deeply submerged in the lives of *adult children* of alcoholics.

What are some feelings common to codependents or coalcoholics?

Anger arises in a love-hate relationship because codependents can't separate the person from the disease. Many have a very hard time working effectively with the distinction between the alcoholic's person and his conduct. Often, moral training in the home and church keeps codependents bound to the conviction that all the alcoholic has to do to change is want or decide to do so — that it is a simple question of willpower.

Shame grows out of embarrassing episodes and inability to control inappropriate drinking. To be out of control is nearly the worst thing that can happen to believers in the Lord Jesus. Christians assume they can do all things through prayer and faith in Jesus Christ. But flesh remains to thwart Christian growth, and few church members are sufficiently open and honest to admit to this specific spiritual conundrum. In their powerlessness, they feel worthless and ashamed.

Hurt feelings fester into bitter arguments, deteriorating health, neglect, abuse, and loss of love.

Fear is spawned in the presence of unreliable relationships, times of verbal abuse, and increasing financial insecurity.

Loneliness shuts off meaningful communication. Unloved and without nurture, everyone in the sad alcoholic drama becomes isolated, cut off, and depressingly introverted.

Is the codependent responsible for the alcoholic's sickness?

No! Problems in marriage, stresses in the workplace, and all other common ills do not produce alcoholism. Spouses especially, and sometimes even innocent children, are made to feel guilty by the manipulating alcoholic. All codependents must come to know beyond the shadow of a doubt that they are not responsible for the alcoholism that disturbs their family. Secure in this knowledge, they can begin to exercise detached love, which is one of the first steps in the codependent's healing process.

Is it prudent for a codependent to drink with an alcoholic who is still in denial?

No. Love for the sick drinker demands action. One way to break his denial is to set an example of chemical freedom. Freedom, contentment, and peace without the use of alcohol send a powerful unspoken message to the alcoholic. Such serenity increases his pain level.

Why do codependents need outside help?

Codependents are out of touch with the facts of their own lives. They fail to see how personal defenses keep the self locked up in hostility, self-pity, anger, and loneliness. They have unwittingly become part of the disease.

How can objective, concerned Christians help and support codependents?

Subject to manipulation, misrepresentation, and the unpredictable behavior of the alcoholic, the codependent often loses self-confidence and questions his or her perception of reality. A third objective person helps the codependent regain perspective and inner strength.

Those who wish to help codependents can:

1. Encourage the codependent to express openly, without restraint, his or her bad feelings.
2. Listen carefully, avoiding superficial and ineffective phrases (e.g., "I know how you feel" [unless the person truly does by virtue of having been through a similar situation], "Your spouse [or parent, or whoever] can't help it," "Christians must try to love the unlovely," or "You just need to pray [or trust, or love] more").
3. Attend Al-Anon meetings with the codependent rather than merely urging attendance. True, godly empathy demands action.
4. Help the person locate professional counselors or caregivers, and help him make connections with these people.

What are the certain fundamentals codependents must learn in order to recover?

There are three. First, coalcoholics need knowledge of the disease of alcoholism. Second, they need to assess personal needs, working toward inner strength capable of tough love. Third, they must learn courage — the courage to risk rejection, anger, and misunderstanding. Spouses, parents, sisters, brothers, and children hurt by alcoholism experience distorted emotions and become helplessly enmeshed in the alcoholic's warped life — so enmeshed, they ignore personal needs.

What is an enabler?

An enabler can be a child, spouse, friend, coworker, clergyman, doctor — anyone who unwittingly enables the alcoholic to continue drinking. A good example of an enabler would be the woman whose husband has gotten sick from drinking and has passed out on the floor at 3:00 A.M. Not only does she clean up the mess and put him into bed, but she sets the clock for 6:00 A.M. so that she can call his boss with an excuse for his absence from work.

Enablers try to help, but they usually go about it in the wrong way. Excuses, covering up, denying the existence of alcoholism, even assuming responsibilities for the alcoholic, are a few examples of enabling. While the codependent may think he is being helpful, he is only postponing the alcoholic's *inevitable* facing up to the reality of his addiction. An enabler may justify the alcoholic's drinking by attributing his drinking to his stressful job, or to the fact that he must lunch daily with people who drink. Any action that shields the alcoholic from experiencing the painful consequences of his drinking enables him to continue to drink and slide deeper into confusion and finally death.

Enablers are codependents. The degree of personal involvement, the nature and intensity of the personal relationship between an enabler and the alcoholic, determines the extent of negative dependency an enabler displays. In other words, a spouse, child, or parent is more codependent than an employer or a friend.

Is enabling love all bad?

Enabling actions are negative; they only result in continued and deepening problems. But the enabler should never be labeled as bad. Too often enablers get bad press. Usually they act the way they do because they have been taught that "loving" people are accepting, encouraging, and helpful. Families are *supposed* to take care of their own. Society actually encourages and praises the super-responsibility of caretakers, especially females. Women are expected to nurture, not abandon. Men are expected to protect, not expose. The enabler is simply working to meet the standards of society — and of the church — where often very little is known about the realities of alcoholism.

Doesn't Christian love require one to help?

Yes. But enabling isn't Christian love, regardless of how it may look. Enabling "love" is not honest love; it conceals, covers up, perpetuates the lie of normality. Because it refuses to acknowledge reality, it only cultivates an environment in which the disease of alcoholism can continue to grow.

How can one stop enabling?

The best way is to learn detachment. Do not feel guilty about past enabling efforts that were motivated by love. Remember that when one lives with an addicted person, one must learn tough love. It is time to be tough, not tender; strong, not compliant. It is time to intervene positively, not hide negatively. It is time to learn detachment.

What is detachment?

Detachment is often called "tough love." Tough love does not mean careless disregard or angry denunciation. Detachment is accepting the fact that the codependent cannot fix the alcoholic's drinking. He backs away from emotional attachment to the alcoholic while he tries to learn about alcoholic illness. Feelings of frustration, fear, anger, and guilt are sorted out gradually. The detached person starts to care in a new way.

Detached love is strong and risks rejection. It patiently keeps on loving. It is hopeful that healing can be found. Detached love allows the alcoholic to experience the ugly results of his drinking. Detached love releases the alcoholic to the hands of God, with the assurance that he catches everyone so released. Detached love is a releasing love that never lets the alcoholic go. It is a strange and blessed paradox.

Why must the enabler learn detachment?

1. The alcoholic must learn to live with the painful consequences of his drinking. To enable him to continue to drink prevents this.
2. The enabler must detach in order to handle feelings of disappointment, frustration, and failure which arise from one's inability to "fix" the alcoholic's life.

What kinds of persons experience the most difficulty learning detachment?

1. Persons who are extremely conscientious, often giving attention to the needs of others while neglecting personal needs.

2. People who view life in terms of do's and don'ts. These regulation-dominated persons tend to ignore and deprecate personal feelings and emotional needs.
3. Rigid persons who seem to be incapable of openly considering alternative ways of thinking and feeling.

FIVE
INTERVENTION

What is intervention?

Intervention is the honest and objective presentation of facts to the alcoholic by concerned persons. Intervention is presenting reality in a *receivable* way to someone out of touch with it. Even if the alcoholic were willing to report the facts, he does not possess the facts to give. He requires more than a one-on-one dialogue.

The shame-filled alcoholic is burdened with guilt; he desperately needs self-affirmation. In a one-on-one dialogue, he instinctively and cleverly manipulates the conversation to his own advantage. He uses humor, "righteous" anger ("What are you talking about? I only get drunk once in a while"), meek compliance ("You're right. I'll do better"), or hurt silence. A team of caring interveners can detect these manipulative strategies faster than an individual. Remember, one must never underestimate the cunning—whether instinctive or intentional—of an alcoholic.

Is intervention primarily a moral confrontation?

No. Caring persons easily make a mistake at this point. They regard intervention as a moral confrontation between Christians. Intervention deals with sickness, not with moral issues. Granted, there are moral issues involved in actions which take place in an intervention, but it is not a moral or religious dialogue. Moral problems can be dealt with only after the drinker has become alcohol-free. Alcoholics do not understand why they are morally confused. Usually they are too sick spiritually to make appropriate moral judgments.

Who performs the intervention?

Four or five caring persons are selected by a professional as an intervention team. The key person is a family member who knows the facts intimately. This key person assists the professional in selecting other team members. The entire team studies to learn the facts of alcoholism as a disease. Team members are "significant others" — siblings, children, spouse, parents, clergy, close friends, anyone respected by the alcoholic. All are carefully prepared for the eventual intervention.

What is meant by the term "significant other"?

This is the person whom the alcoholic views as being very important to his life. The significant other may be a spouse, an employer, or a friend. Usually this significant person becomes the *effective catalyst* to help the alcoholic accept the reality of his powerlessness and need for help.

How do interveners integrate moral issues into their work?

The immediate goal of treatment for an alcoholic is abstinence. Abstinence by family members often helps the alcoholic achieve and maintain sobriety. The goal of abstinence is communicated best by focusing on the primary and progressive nature of the disease.

At this point it is not prudent or appropriate to discuss moral and religious motivations. Most likely alcohol abuse has produced profound religious and moral dysfunction. By the time of the intervention the alcoholic is often in late-stage alcoholism, entrenched in denial, and unable to engage in religious and moral discussions. The spiritual dimensions in the alcoholic's life were the first to be seriously impaired. The first goal, then, should be to separate the alcoholic from the drug. This often requires detoxification and inpatient treatment.

We are not suggesting that moral issues are irrelevant. There are many alcohol-related events that come to the forefront. For

example, there may have been a driving violation. There may
have been blatant marital infidelity. Perhaps intervention must
be weighted in favor of these moral issues, but it must be re-
membered that these events for which the *late-stage alcoholic* is
responsible must be confronted on a different level than moral
dialogue between two Christians. He is already burdened with
guilt! He simply can't act with moral sensitivity. It is counter-
productive to address him as if his inappropriate behavior were
a sin of volition (an act of the conscious will). Instead, God's
people must make decisions for him and lead him into ways of
treatment and healing.

What specific preparations are made by the intervention team?

They visit open AA, Al-Anon, and Alateen meetings. (See
Section Four of Part Three for an explanation of these groups.)
They are taught to be empathetic, to enter into the feeling levels
of the alcoholic. They learn about rationalization, projection,
denial, fear, loss of self-esteem, guilt, and other psycho-social
dynamics. They learn these things primarily by listening to
people talk and share at meetings.

They are taught to make specific lists of the alcoholic's behavior. Facts are coherently and concisely written down. These
lists of specific inappropriate behavior are read sensitively and
objectively at the time of the intervention. During the reading at
the intervention, the alcoholic is not permitted to comment, or
to treat the lists as an occasion for disagreement and argument.

Interventions require careful planning and preparation. Hast-
ily called and ill-prepared interventions fail. A fumbled intervention does more harm than good, driving the alcoholic deeper
into the bottle and codependents deeper into frustration, shame,
and despair.

What takes place during an intervention?

The chairperson, usually a knowledgeable, emotionally
stable, and objective professional, sets the ground rules for the
procedure. The alcoholic is asked to listen, not respond. If he in-
terrupts, objects, argues, or tries to take charge, the chairperson

firmly resists. Only after all the lists have been read does the chairperson invite the alcoholic's comments.

The lists recall specific incidents. Instead of saying, "I think you are drinking more now than you did in the past," one would state, "The last four Saturday night dinners were unpleasant because your speech was slurred, and embarrassingly loud. Last week you told a story that was obscene. When I mentioned the story to you the next day, you denied ever having told it. You couldn't even remember what you had said." Careful, accurate evaluations of behavior—judgments if you will—are made by speaking the truth in love.

What is meant by the phrase "hitting bottom"?

The point at which each alcoholic hits bottom is different. Included in hitting bottom are the following:

1. The alcoholic experiences a painful, traumatic situation as a result of his drinking. This can be just about anything: bad health news after a physical examination; a spouse or child leaves home; loss of one's job; a DWI automobile accident; anything causing intense pain.

2. The alcoholic's family and friends allow this pain to remain sharp, unrelieved, and constant. Pain often breaks the drinker's willful delusion, "I can handle alcohol." It's true—pain is the alcoholic's best friend.

3. The hurting, helpless alcoholic reaches beyond himself in an act of trusting surrender. Christians know from experience that Jesus Christ graciously puts back together a life that is broken, and soothes the pain of many wounds. He still chooses the weak, the despised, and the broken. In this work of redeeming love, he often uses people to help people.

4. The alcoholic lets go and lets God take over. Healing and recovery begin precisely at this point.

An intervention made knowledgeably, patiently, and compassionately creates pain, displays tough love, and creates a situation in which it is safe for the alcoholic to hit bottom. When the pain of continuing to drink alcohol is greater than the pain of not drinking, treatment becomes a real choice for the alcoholic.

What is the difference between honest judgment and judgmentalism?

There are two ways of making judgments. The first, judgmentalism, breathes a negative spirit. It talks down to people from a position of superiority. It alienates, rejects, condemns, and puts hurting persons on the defensive. Rules are more important than people. Hurting, wayward people are "proven wrong" and the accuser is vindicated in his righteousness.

Honest judgment, on the other hand, breathes a positive spirit of empathy arising out of sensitive concern for the person being evaluated. Honest evaluations are more than correct statements of fact. These judgments are positive, accepting, caring, and person-directed. Even if biblical moral standards have been violated, the person is made to feel accepted, cared for, and worthy of love. Sin is rejected, but never the sinner! Practices are openly criticized, but the person is embraced by accepting love.

In an intervention where honest judgments are made, the spirit of Christ must be evident. There must be understanding, compassion, acceptance, encouragement, and hope. Interveners make alcoholics visibly uncomfortable, but they do so in the spirit of Jesus.

How did Jesus avoid judgmentalism?

In his conversation with the Samaritan woman (John 4:7-26) he was accepting, open, and sympathetic before he mentioned her marital problems. In John 8:3-11, he silently protected the adulterous woman, wrote in the sand, and dismissed her detractors before he said, "Go and sin no more." His eyes radiated an accepting look toward Peter in the confusion of his denials. He was patient with his disciples in the upper room who wanted first place in the Messianic kingdom.

The spirit of the Good Shepherd must be radiantly present in the entire intervention process.

What is the best location for an intervention?

Circumstances often dictate location. A place should be chosen where the alcoholic will feel least threatened: his home, the home of his best friend, a professional counselor's office, or even the alcoholic's own office at his place of business. The pastor's study, because it symbolizes religious authority, is probably a poor choice. The alcoholic is afraid of religious authority because of his overwhelming guilt.

What is the place of prayer at an intervention?

The Holy Spirit will give guidance as to whether a formal audible prayer is appropriate at this time. One question to ask is whether the alcoholic is too sick and confused for it to make sense to pray with him. The question does not imply that understanding must accompany prayer for the act to be acceptable to God and effective. Anyone who has prayed for a comatose patient and seen the miracle of instant healing knows better! This question concerns the intervention scene, which often is charged with high emotion, great pain, and extreme tension.

Prayer is the essential ingredient for healing. The team during all its time of preparation will place the sick person in the hands of the Lord, our Healer. The intervention creates the framework in which the healing Spirit of Christ moves. He moves through factual presentations, caring persons, painful tears, insightful comments, patient silences, angry outbursts, and sudden unspoken prayers.

Powerlessness is the key word in an intervention. Both the alcoholic and caring interveners are powerless over alcohol. Into this powerlessness comes the healing, powerful Lord. He heals frustrated and hurt interveners, as well as the alcoholic. Jesus' Spirit moves sovereignly and makes plain, in his own way, whether or not a formal audible prayer is appropriate. Trust him. He is always way ahead of us with his blessing.

How does the intervention end?

The team has agreed on a course of action prior to the intervention. In fact, the alcoholic's suitcase is packed, a bed reserved, a counselor selected, a vehicle and driver waiting; everything is ready for what all involved hope will happen: the alcoholic's recognition of his problem and subsequent decision to seek help. These matters have been decided during the careful planning stages before the intervention.

Sometimes the alcoholic angrily exits, making the intervention appear to have failed. This is disappointing. It happens no matter how carefully the team has prepared and cooperated, or how skillfully the chairperson has functioned.

Angry exits do not mean that the intervention has failed. It merely has failed to reach its *immediate* goal. Everyone has learned. The team, and especially the alcoholic, will never be the same. The "unsuccessful" intervention has become part of the healing process. Love is patient, believing all things, hoping all things. The Lord is in control!

An intervention also may conclude with the alcoholic reluctantly consenting to go into treatment. There may be sullen anger, which may last a while. But wait. Have patience. The sick do become healthy, and anger eventually will turn into gratitude.

Sensitive interveners try to restore the damaged self-esteem of the alcoholic. He may choose another route to health. The team will respect his wishes and deal kindly with promises, even though they have been made in weakness. With strength and empathetic love, each team member will try to help the sick person make the best choice. The team will remember that its choice is not the only road to recovery. Here too, life is an adventure! Risk taking is part of loving. Let the Lord's Spirit take the lead.

How can the Christian community help facilitate intervention?

Churches are healing communities. Members can be recruited for a special ministry to the broken lives involved in alcoholism. Many congregations have organized and trained Family Outreach Teams that are ready to serve those who are in the grip of chemical dependency.

What is a Family Outreach Team?

It is a team of five to twenty caring members who are commissioned by the congregation to carry on a special ministry to families impacted by alcoholism and codependency. The team is designed to help those in the church and community.

Members of a Family Outreach Team are trained for at least

six months before they serve on the team. They train to gain knowledge about alcoholism and chemical dependencies, to understand the problems of codependency, to learn the art of listening, and to know how to identify agencies and people in the community who can help. Team members learn to deal with denial, to lower barriers of shame, to reduce burdens of guilt, and to provide support for those caught in the confusing world of addiction and codependency. They practice the principles of anonymity and confidentiality, which are vital in creating a relationship of trust and confidence. They also learn detachment, understanding they can "fix" no one. Teams do not diagnose or practice counseling, but they bring people and professionals together.

Usually a team meets twice a month for two hours to refresh their training. They read updated materials, watch films, listen to lectures, visit treatment centers, and attend open AA, Al-Anon, and Alateen meetings.

An excellent guide for creating Family Outreach Teams is *The Training Manual,* by Dr. Richard E. Grevengoed, Executive Director of the Christian Care Center (2325 177th St., Lansing, Illinois, 60438, 708-895-7310 or 1-800-248-7060).

Are there Bible passages to help interveners?

Yes. Paul clearly states how Christians, directed by God's love, should present themselves to others. "Do not let any unwholesome talk come out of your mouths, but only what is helpful for building others up according to their needs, that it may benefit those who listen. . . . Get rid of all bitterness, rage and anger, brawling and slander, along with every form of malice. Be kind and compassionate to one another, forgiving each other, just as in Christ God forgave you" (Ephesians 4:29, 31-32).

When an alcoholic turns his will and life over to God, he desperately needs a loving and accepting fellowship to help him. Far too many recovering alcoholics report that they received fellowship and understanding from AA, but that the church fellowship remained closed to their deep needs for understanding and healing. The need for healing discipleship is as urgent now as it was in the perilous times experienced by the New Testament churches.

SIX
THE CHURCH'S
INVOLVEMENT

Are there many families with alcohol problems in the church community?

There are more alcoholics in the Christian community than most people realize. One out of 7 drinkers slides into alcoholism. This is as true for the Christian community as it is for those outside of it. Because of willful and complacent ignorance of the facts of this disease, Christian families in deep trouble are not getting the help they urgently need.

What positive suggestions are there to help codependents?

1. Don't start with the alcoholic! Rather, get all the facts you can absorb about alcoholism. Study this disease.

2. Attend open AA meetings, Al-Anon meetings, and other alcohol/drug related community and church programs. Try not to worry about being seen by others at these meetings.

3. Recognize that you are emotionally involved. Self-examination and open discussion with trusted friends and your pastor are necessary. Don't become disheartened. Alcoholism has taken a long time to develop and recovery will not happen overnight. Do not be surprised at broken promises and relapses. Continue to take care of yourself.

4. Approach the alcoholic only when he is sober. Speak to him when he is hung over, shortly after being drunk, while he is suffering remorse and depression.

5. Work at detachment. Get beyond reactive behavior. Be objective, reporting facts as calmly and objectively as possible.

6. Explain the nature of alcoholic illness to children. Try to spare them the trauma of seeing their parent intoxicated. Advise local police and even bartenders of the situation if you feel this might help prevent harmful and embarrassing incidents.

7. Find an Al-Anon sponsor (see Part Three, Section Two) to help you practice the difficult art of detachment. "Let go and let God" is not an easy concept or action. Thank God for gifted persons who are willing and able to help. Keep looking until you find a compatible sponsor.

What are some negative things to avoid?
1. Don't moralize, nag, lecture, or preach. Even emotional appeals ("If you love me . . . ") are ineffective. Though such actions are most understandable, they wrongly assume that the alcoholic is able to control his drinking.

2. Don't allow the drinker to outsmart or manipulate you. This will only encourage his avoidance of responsibility and diminish his respect for you.

3. Avoid extracting promises that are sure to be broken. Pledges, readily given and quickly shattered, intensify feelings of guilt and shame. To handle this pain, the alcoholic will drink. His drinking will increase inner pain which will lead to more drinking. His life will sink deeper into the swamp of confusion and despair.

4. Do not cover up or make excuses for the alcoholic. This is extremely difficult for family members who are financially dependent on the drinker's income. Learn about employee assistance programs.

5. Never use children as weapons to "get to" the alcoholic. Avoid the temptation to play the long-suffering martyr. Don't nurse that seething pot of anger. Remember, you are the alcoholic's best source of help and hope.

6. Use common sense, seek outside help, and learn to act now. Alcoholism only gets worse. Although it may seem to go

away temporarily, it does not. To do nothing is the worst choice
to make. Unaddressed, this illness ends in insanity or death.

How can pastors, elders, and other church leaders be equipped to deal with alcoholism in their churches and beyond?

The qualifications mentioned in 1 Timothy 3:1-7 and Titus
1:5-9 are precisely those needed to handle the many problems
one meets when confronting alcoholism. Timothy and Titus
remind us that elders, pastors, and all servant-leaders in the
church are to be "temperate, self-controlled, able to teach, not
given to much wine themselves, gentle, not quarrelsome, and
not a recent convert." Attitudes born out of "not given to much
wine" help one look objectively at personal decisions to drink
or abstain. "Being able to teach" implies knowledge of alcoholism and its complex, confusing, and powerful character. To nurture alcoholics and their families demands gentle sensitivity.
Finally, the maturity that comes from "not being a recent convert" prepares one to wait for change patiently with persever-
ance and prayer.

What if the alcoholic refuses help?

If the alcoholic continues in his denial and refuses help, the
focus of the spiritual leaders should shift to the family. Their
attitudes and actions have been painfully influenced by the alcoholic's behavior. They need help. They are called coalcoholics
not because they drink, but because their lives have been
twisted out of shape by alcoholism.

Should persistently willful alcoholics in denial be removed from church membership?

Formal Christian discipline, exercised faithfully, is an essential factor in healthy Christian growth. Leaders must press the
claims of Christ upon church members. Church discipline under
the authority of Jesus is a matter of *discipling* a member of
Christ's family.

The goal of church discipline is not excommunication, which
is formal separation from the fellowship in the name of Christ.
The goal of disciplinary action is *redemption, restoration,* and

reclamation. Persons estranged from fellowship are sought out with compassion, the kind displayed by the shepherd who leaves the ninety-and-nine safe and risks everything to find the lost one. *The "lost," when found, can easily sense whether the "finder" comes with the spirit of compassion or of condemnation.*

Sadly, termination of church membership sometimes does happen — but the act of termination should come only after a long period of patient loving. If the alcoholic persistently refuses to seek help for his disease, termination of certain privileges and relationships may be necessary for the welfare of the church's spiritual health, and especially for the spiritual welfare of the alcoholic and his family. Even as an employer does not fire an employee for having a disease, but for willful refusal to get help, so the Christian community does not bar a person from fellowship because of a disease, but because of refusal to get help. The critical point at issue is willful refusal to get help. Such refusal may precipitate formal disciplinary proceedings.

Notice the use of the word "may." This word has been chosen advisedly, not because we wish to minimize the responsibility to exercise formal discipline, nor because the alcoholic is beyond functioning as a responsible Christian. Alcoholism is cunning, baffling, and powerful. A person may become so chemically twisted in his perception of reality that he must be treated as being mentally deranged. The chronic alcoholic is beyond cognitive functioning and is incapable of making a moral decision. He is unable to receive or refuse helpful intervention. Therefore the disciplinary process must proceed slowly. Adjudication should take place carefully. What will happen is that the alcoholic will inevitably receive the help he needs and return to the community of believers, or he will continue to drink. While waiting for healing, God's people must pray and rely on his mercy.

Church members must take the same steps as the recovering alcoholic. The first step is this: *Admit we are powerless over our brother's alcoholism and that we are not able to manage his life.* It is our calling to do what we can, and then turn him over to God, whose judgment is gracious and whose graciousness is just.

PART THREE

Journey Into Recovery

ONE: Treatment Programs

At what point does recovery from alcoholism begin? ◆ What treatment options are available for the alcoholic? ◆ Which treatment option is the most effective? ◆ How intensive is an inpatient treatment program? ◆ What takes place in an inpatient treatment program? ◆ What is the unique focus of effective alcoholism treatment? ◆ What help is available for families of alcoholics and codependents?

TWO: Alcoholics Anonymous (AA)

What is Alcoholics Anonymous? ◆ What are some misconceptions people have about AA? ◆ How did AA get started? ◆ Is AA a religious society? ◆ What does AA mean by "spirituality"? ◆ What spiritual lessons are learned in AA? ◆ Does AA have a formal creed? ◆ How do alcoholics attain sobriety in AA? ◆ What are the Twelve Steps of AA? ◆ What are AA meetings? ◆ What is an AA sponsor? ◆ Why is it important for a recovering person to relate to a sponsor? ◆ What specific problems does an AA member discuss with his sponsor? ◆ How does AA deal with shame and guilt? ◆ Why do most AA members treat the psychiatric approach to alcoholism as suspect and ineffective? ◆ Why do many AA members have problems with religion, clergy, and the church? ◆ Why do alcoholics relapse?

THREE: Al-Anon and Alateen

What is Al-Anon? ◆ What is Alateen? ◆ Why are AA, Al-Anon, and Alateen separate fellowships?

FOUR: AA and the Church

How does AA help Christians deal with alcoholism? ◆ Must the Christian alcoholic witness at his AA meeting? ◆ Why do many Christians carefully follow the AA program? ◆ Is the course language often used by those attending AA meetings an obstacle for alcoholic Christians? ◆ Should recovering alcoholics who are Christians create their own meetings? ◆ Do many Christians experience confusion when going to regular AA meetings? ◆ Have meetings been designed which are specifically Christian in focus? ◆ What types of treatments are used in such groups? ◆ Are Christian groups effective?

FIVE: Christians and Recovery

Are alcoholics instantaneously delivered (cured) in religious conversion? ◆ What are some steps a church can take to develop educational programs regarding alcoholism and codependency? ◆ Why does the phrase "in Christ" hold special meaning for those in recovery? ◆ How do Christians often underestimate and restrict Christ's work in recovery? ◆ How do freedom, rules, and love relate in a Bible-directed life-style?

SIX: Aftercare

What are aftercare groups? ◆ Why are aftercare groups essential for recovery? ◆ What recovery pitfalls are often

83

discussed in aftercare? ◆ What is a peculiar danger for
Christians in aftercare sessions? ◆ What is a pre-condition
for helping others in recovery? ◆ What short formula can
be used for self-appraisal?

Appendix A: Christian Recovery Groups
Suggested Format and Topics ◆ Variations on AA's Twelve
Steps ◆ Personal Attitude Index

Appendix B: Resources
Books ◆ Films ◆ National Organizations

85

ONE
TREATMENT PROGRAMS

At what point does recovery from alcoholism begin?

It begins at the point when the alcoholic seeks help from outside sources. The alcoholic hits bottom. This need not be the point of complete family, social, financial, and physical ruin. Many recovering persons experience a relatively "high bottom," one involving little loss. The purpose of intervention is to create a high bottom, presenting the reality of an intolerable life situation in a way that can be accepted by the alcoholic. (See pages 69ff.)

What treatment options are available for the alcoholic?

Basically, there are four treatment options:

1. An inpatient treatment program at a local hospital or at another alcohol/drug treatment center.
2. An outpatient treatment program at a local hospital or at another alcohol/drug treatment center.
3. A private course of treatment with a professional alcoholism/addiction counselor.
4. Joining AA, working the Twelve-Step program daily (see page 91), and attending meetings regularly.

Which treatment option is the most effective?

Because alcoholism displays itself in so many forms, this can be answered only on an individual, case-by-case basis in consultation with an experienced, licensed, Christian counselor. The twenty-eight-day inpatient treatment program is the most intensive, carefully supervised, and family-oriented program of treatment.

How intensive is an inpatient treatment program?

It usually takes twenty-eight days in a hospital or treatment center. It normally involves all members of the family at some appropriate time and is always followed by supervised outpatient aftercare. Programs at accredited institutions usually are covered by health insurance.

What takes place in an inpatient treatment program?

1. Detoxification, under medical supervision if necessary.
2. Complete physical and psychological assessments.
3. Group therapy involving interaction with fellow alcoholics under the direction of a professional counselor.
4. Occupational and recreational therapy.
5. Intensive education about the disease dynamics of alcoholism.
6. Involvement with Alcoholics Anonymous (AA) with special emphasis on its spiritual dimensions.
7. Treatment of the alcoholic family's dysfunctions.

What is the unique focus of effective alcoholism treatment?

Effective alcoholism treatment involves a tricky paradox. On the one hand, alcoholism is a biochemical disease arising out of a special genetic predisposition. On the other hand, effective treatment focuses clearly on the spiritual and moral dimensions of the alcoholic.

This paradox underscores some noteworthy facts. A recovering alcoholic is never so healed or healthy that he can safely return to using alcohol. He *remains* alcoholic. From what is known today, the biochemical characteristics of the alcoholic do not change during effective treatment. There is no immunizing serum or antibiotic that erases or neutralizes the alcoholic's biochemistry and metabolism. Loss of control over alcohol is always latent and is reactivated when drinking resumes.

For this reason we speak of *recovering* alcoholics, not *recovered, cured,* or *healed* alcoholics. Recovery demands abstinence. God's gift of healing delivers the alcoholic from active, compulsive drinking, not from the biochemical, metabolic processes which are unique to him.

Careful distinctions at this point are necessary. If a recovering alcoholic imagines himself as recovered, able to drink moderately again, he is taking the first step downward into his former bondage. He is "put together" in such a way that alcohol always adversely twists his spiritual and moral control centers. Maturing spiritual and moral perspectives help the alcoholic handle his special limits. The paradox of a physiological disease being treated with spiritual and moral emphases must never be resolved by intellectual efforts to try to "figure things out." Healing is the work of God's grace as it works in a person's life, bringing moral and spiritual growth.

What help is available for families of alcoholics and codependents?

Al-Anon and Alateen are the best known groups available to help codependents and families of alcoholics. (See page 97.)

TWO
ALCOHOLICS
ANONYMOUS (AA)

What is Alcoholics Anonymous?

The following two-paragraph definition, which is read at many group meetings, is perhaps the best description of AA:

"Alcoholics Anonymous is a fellowship of men and women who share their experience, strength, and hope with each other that they may solve their common problem and help others to recover from alcoholism.

"The only requirement for membership is a desire to stop drinking. There are no dues or fees for AA membership: we are self-supporting through our own contributions. AA is not allied with any sect, denomination, politics, organization, or institution; does not wish to engage in any controversy; neither endorses nor opposes any causes. Our primary purpose is to stay sober and help other alcoholics to achieve sobriety."

What are some misconceptions people have about AA?

Some hesitate to recommend or use AA because they picture the fellowship as a collection of derelicts and uneducated bums who sit in smoke-filled rooms swapping "war stories." This is far from the truth. Those who attend AA meetings represent every classification of society. To go to AA is to meet a next-door neighbor, a member of a church, a doctor, or even a minister.

Information about AA meetings in any area can be found by dialing the numbers found in the yellow pages of the phone book.

How did AA get started?

AA was founded in 1935 in Akron, Ohio, by two men identified only as Bill W., a former New York stockbroker, and Dr. Bob S., an Akron surgeon. Both seemingly hopeless alcoholics discovered they could strengthen their own sobriety by sharing it with others.

Is AA a religious society?

No, AA is not a religious society or movement in a church. Its recovery program includes suggestions that reflect the insights of many spiritual leaders.

What does AA mean by "spirituality"?

For a non-Christian alcoholic, it means openness to new ways of seeing life. It is *teachableness* or docility. Spirituality is receiving help from outside the self in order to live serenely without alcohol. By consciously remaining open and receptive to new spiritual influences, the member is lifted out of the morass of alcoholism.

For the Christian in AA, it means openness to the work of Jesus Christ in the Spirit. The Holy Spirit uses the experiences of other recovering persons. He delivers alcoholics out of the prison of despair and hopelessness. Spirituality begins with acknowledging that Jesus Christ meets one in the stories of recovering people as well as in the words of holy Scripture.

Recovering persons seek out meetings where their unique needs are best met. They eagerly receive the insights of others, sift them, accept or reject them, and use the insights that are personally helpful. AA openness is impatient with religious people who are rigidly convinced that they alone are right.

Spirituality is a special blend of willingness, honesty, humility, and humor. Eleventh-step meetings (see page 92) are places where one discovers this kind of spirituality.

What spiritual lessons are learned in AA?

By sharing spiritual experiences, members learn how to deal with self-centeredness, pride, illusions of control, quick gratification of desires, resentment, fear, guilt, shame, disregard of others, and other defects of daily life. The lessons learned are specific, practical, and usually painful. AA members learn to live honestly with a *fragile* and *limited* humanness which admits to repeated failures and the need for daily help.

Does AA have a formal creed?

No. AA members are not required to accept any formal statement or creed. They need only admit that they have a drinking problem, that they desire to stop and want help. A unifying and overarching conviction of AA members is the faith that a recovering alcoholic, by sharing his experience, can be effective in helping other alcoholics.

How do alcoholics attain sobriety in AA?

Through the example and friendship of the recovering alcoholics in AA, new members are encouraged to stay away from drinking "one day at a time." AA's members concentrate on not drinking now — today.

New members also learn to follow a program of twelve steps, which simply state the experience of an estimated one million men and women who have been able to remain sober through their use. They are encouraged to attend meetings at which they can share their alcohol-related experiences with one another.

What are the Twelve Steps of AA?

1. We admitted that we were powerless over alcohol — that our lives had become unmanageable.
2. We came to believe that a power greater than ourselves could restore us to sanity.
3. We made a decision to turn our will and our lives over to the care of God, *as we understood him.*
4. We made a searching and fearless moral inventory of ourselves.
5. We admitted to God, to ourselves, and to another human being the exact nature of our wrongs.

6. We were entirely ready to have God remove all these defects of character.

7. We humbly asked him to remove our shortcomings.

8. We made a list of all persons we had harmed, and became willing to make amends to them all.

9. We made direct amends to such people whenever possible, except when to do so would injure them or others.

10. We continued to take personal inventory, and when we were wrong, promptly admitted it.

11. We sought through prayer and meditation to improve our conscious contact with God, *as we understood him,* praying only for knowledge of his will for us and the power to carry that out.

12. Having had a spiritual awakening as a result of these steps, we tried to carry this message to alcoholics and to practice these principles in all our affairs.

What are AA meetings?

Alcoholics Anonymous is made up of more than 42,000 local groups in 110 countries. The people in each group get together, usually once or twice a week, to hold AA meetings which are of two types:

1. At *open meetings* speakers tell how they drank, how they discovered AA, and how its program has helped them. Relatives and friends are welcome at open meetings.

2. *Closed meetings* are for alcoholics only. These are group discussions during which any member may speak. At closed AA meetings members can get help with personal problems that arise from the effort to stay sober one day at a time.

What is an AA sponsor?

A sponsor is a trusted recovering alcoholic of the same sex, who is always available for help to the alcoholic who asks for his services. The sponsor has had several years of serene sobriety. His experiential knowledge is an immediate and urgently needed part of recovery.

Why is it important for a recovering person to relate to a sponsor?

Early in recovery, and with repeated intensity, the compulsion to drink again rears its attractive but deadly head. When this urge becomes overwhelmingly strong, when abstinence seems about to disappear, the recovering alcoholic needs a trusted, experienced friend to intervene with clear advice, tough love, and empathetic concern.

What specific problems does an AA member discuss with his sponsor?

One example is resentment, the desire to balance accounts for real or imagined hurts by getting angry, sulking, or lashing out. The AA member will write out a personal inventory and share it with a sponsor. This involves answering in detail such questions as, "Whom do I respect?" "What caused the resentment I feel?" "How does my resentment affect my self-esteem, physical well-being, or moods?" "Does my resentment color my evaluation of others?" "What am I doing to rid my life of this resentment?" AA members deal in a similar fashion with such things as fear, guilt, shame, pride, intolerance, phoniness, greed, self-pity, procrastination, and much more.

Taking a personal and honest inventory and sharing it with a sponsor is a painful experience. It should be ongoing — and here is where many Christians in recovery fail. They have stopped drinking, but they fail to continue the process of healing and understanding what has happened — and is still happening — inside of them as a result of the drinking. "Search me, O God, and know my heart; test my thoughts" (Psalm 139:23, TLB) is an honest prayer for those who are working the Fourth and Fifth Steps of AA.

How does AA deal with shame and guilt?

Troubled people deal with common problems and learn to accept personal limitations with honesty and openness. At a typical sharing session in AA, one might hear something like this: "I really did not wish to drink when I did drink!"

Someone replies, "Of course! You didn't want to drink, but

you did! You drink because you're an alcoholic, not because you're weak-willed or morally flawed. Accept your limitation. We're radically powerless when we ingest alcohol. Don't forget it! Especially today, right now!"

Similar honesty is discovered among codependents in groups such as Al-Anon and Alateen, which practice the Twelve-Step program.

Guilt is not ignored. In these meetings, members honestly and freely talk about defects of character and deeds which hurt loved ones. Personal inventory is serious business. Lists are made, often together with a trusted AA sponsor (see previous question). Generalizations like "We're all sinners" don't count with AA. Many are ready to have God's help. Honesty and humility are the weapons to defeat shame in the available power of the Holy Spirit. Working the Twelve Steps with Jesus' help is the way to stay serenely sober and lovingly detached. The gift of healing is available to all in Jesus Christ.

Why do most AA members treat the psychiatric approach to alcoholism as suspect and ineffective?

Many psychiatrists consider alcohol problems as symptoms of various underlying mental or emotional disorders. Some even call alcoholism itself a psychiatric disorder.

It is true that either set of problems — psychiatric or alcoholic — *may* occur as a result of the other. Long-term alcohol abuse can produce functional and structural mental disorders. Likewise, people with psychiatric problems sometimes medicate themselves by using alcohol compulsively. Most frequently, however, alcohol addiction and psychiatric problems are independent phenomena, and require different methods of treatment.

Why do many AA members have problems with religion, clergy, and the church?

Alcoholics in denial perceive God as unloving and full of damning wrath. Clergy and church members are viewed as "having it made" when it comes to faith in God. The alcoholic hates himself for "not having it made." Powerlessness and unmanageability over alcohol is his unique limit. Without realizing it, he projects this intense feeling of inadequacy to God, the clergy, and church members.

In AA meetings this self-hatred gradually is uncovered and revealed for what it is. It is seen as pride and grandiosity. But the alcoholic is not criticized, belittled, berated, or ridiculed for his misplaced anger. No one expects him to see things straight. Relating to a higher power is not demanded as a test for membership.

Longtime AA members have slogged through this swamp of self-loathing and anger. They patiently listen, correct, encourage, and help the alcoholic accept himself. Alcoholic conduct is not accepted, but the alcoholic person is. Sober self-acceptance slowly but effectively conquers misperceptions and misplaced anger.

Why do alcoholics relapse?

Relapse (using alcohol again after a time of abstinence) happens because the alcoholic does not work the AA program with honest, daily effort. This is the universal testimony of alcoholics who relapse, return, relapse, and finally persevere into serene sobriety.

Consistently sharing experiences around AA tables helps drinkers keep alcohol out of their lives, giving their bodies, minds, and emotions a chance to get well. To avoid relapse, they begin to clarify confused thinking and avoid unhappy feelings by working AA's Twelve Steps to recovery more diligently. They also stay in touch with other members between meetings to learn how they maintain sobriety.

THREE
AL-ANON AND ALATEEN

What is Al-Anon?

Al-Anon was founded by families of alcoholics. It is a form of group interaction to help those who live with alcoholics. In these groups, those who live with alcoholics learn that they are unable to control the alcoholic's drinking, no matter how hard they try. Members of Al-Anon use the Twelve Steps of AA, along with their own slogans. It is an anonymous and confidential fellowship.

Al-Anon can help build a person's confidence and serenity, which will help that person better deal constructively and decisively with the alcoholic. The group fellowship can help the nonalcoholic parent create a relatively normal environment for nurturing children. Al-Anon can help members reduce anxiety, worry, and guilt. Like AA, it is a nonreligious group of people who face a common, many-faceted problem. (For information on Al-Anon, write Al-Anon Family Group Headquarters, P.O. Box 182, Madison Square Station, New York, N.Y. 10010.)

What is Alateen?

Alateen is a group for young people from ages 12 to 20 who live in an alcoholic family situation. It is an outgrowth of Al-Anon. In Alateen, there is group discussion, sharing of experiences, encouragement, and mutual learning of effective ways to cope with alcoholism as it affects each person's life. In interaction with others, members of Alateen learn to exercise compassion rather than contempt for the alcoholic. They learn to develop some emotional detachment, which helps in the process of maturation. Together, members of Alateen try to build satisfying and rewarding life experiences for themselves. (For information on Alateen, contact the Al-Anon address above.)

Why are AA, Al-Anon, and Alateen separate fellowships?

The problems of alcoholism and codependency are different, though similar. Feelings of confusion, shame, hopelessness, fear, guilt, and so forth are common to members in all three groups. But the roads travelled to reach this misery are distinct. Persons who are journeying on the same road are best able to help each other.

Also, anonymity is the best environment in which to practice openness, honesty, and trust. At least at first, the individual work each member of an alcoholic family must do can seldom be accomplished if other members of the family — especially the alcoholic — are present.

FOUR
AA AND THE CHURCH

How does AA help Christians deal with alcoholism?

AA helps by making available, in story form, the practical experiences of alcoholics who daily learn to live without alcohol. Many Christian intervention teams, as well as many pastors, ask AA members to meet with alcoholics and their families to explain the AA recovery program.

Must the Christian alcoholic witness at his AA meeting?

Jesus Christ is his higher power! No question about this! At meetings one can hear someone say, "Hi! My name is . . . and Jesus Christ is my higher power. He keeps me sober today. I thank him for every one of you, because I learn from your experiences with the program."

Seldom is more said. But this silence is not for reasons of cowardice or shame. Reluctance to press Christ's claims arises out of respect for his presence and authority. Many recovering alcoholics are not ready to understand a Christian's testimony. Spiritual confusions abound at meetings. But after the meeting, over a friendly cup of coffee, the Lord himself creates the opportunity, gives words of simple truth, and reaches out through people to heal others. He's in perfect control!

A compulsive urge to "testify" may arise out of fearful insecurity rather than grateful love. Jesus does not need our words. Indeed, he condescends at times to use our faulty words.

Deliberate silence at an AA meeting may be the ripe fruit of patience rather than the green fruit of fear. When it comes to testifying one must learn the quiet trust of "letting go and letting God." Remaining open to the Spirit is the true way of love and obedience.

Why do many Christians carefully follow the AA program?

AA's Twelve Steps describe recognizable Christian experiences using nonreligious language.

— *powerlessness in finding serenity:* "Grant me a willing spirit, to sustain me" (Psalm 51:12).

—*unmanageability in moral choices:* "I have the desire to do what is good, but I cannot carry it out" (Romans 7:18).

—*complete willingness to have all defects removed:* "I acknowledged my sin to you and did not cover up my iniquity" (Psalm 32:5).

—*making a fearless moral inventory:* "Search me, O God, and know my heart; test me and know my anxious thoughts. See if there is any offensive way in me" (Psalm 139:23-24).

— making amends to those we hurt: "If . . . your brother has something against you . . . go and be reconciled" (Matthew 5:23-24).

—*turning life and will over to God.* "My soul finds rest in God alone; my salvation comes from him" (Psalm 62:1).

—*seeking conscious contact with God:* "Lord, teach us to pray" (Luke 11:1).

—*having had a spiritual awakening, carrying the message:* "O Lord, open my lips, and my mouth will declare your praise" (Psalm 51:15).

Is the coarse language often used by those attending AA meetings an obstacle for alcoholic Christians?

Undesirable language need not be an obstacle. The Christian alcoholic is as confused as any other kind of alcoholic; in fact, he may be more confused, because his compulsive drinking violates many of his deepest religious convictions. Besides, he attends AA meetings to learn daily sobriety, not to receive religious instruction.

AA members urge one another to find a meeting in which they feel comfortable. Offensive language usually can be overcome with patience and sensitivity, without becoming preachy or self-righteous. Recovering alcoholics are not out to offend others. They will try to modify their language when asked. But if this doesn't happen, then AA wisdom advises the member who objects to the language to find another meeting.

Should recovering alcoholics who are Christians create their own meetings?

This may be a good idea. It is obviously true that Christians need to talk openly, insightfully, and humbly about Christ, his teachings, his promises, and his commands. Christ is the *life* of Christians. It is unfair to ask persons who do not have an intimate, personal relationship with Jesus Christ to understand this unique faith relationship. In a typical AA meeting it may be inappropriate to discuss these questions using terms that many do not understand. For these reasons, it sometimes may be necessary for Christians to find a special meeting.

Christians should realize, however, that AA itself provides opportunity for specific religious and spiritual discussions. Eleventh-Step meetings deal with prayer, conscious contact with God, and understanding his will. There is unrestricted opportunity to share openly. Christians continue to learn from each other. In this process many who are still strangers to Christ's love come to hear the genuine gospel for the first time. If special meetings are held, I believe attendance at such meetings should never replace attendance at regular AA meetings.

Do many Christians experience confusion when going to regular AA meetings?

Yes. A few reasons for this are:

1. The AA program is not specifically Christian in orientation, and so is deliberately vague in its Twelve Steps terminology. Its program may contain basic Christian principles, but many Christians believe Christ works most directly in programs that are explicitly biblical in language and approach.

2. Many Christian alcoholics experience basic and rapid deterioration of biblical insight and conduct. The first aspect of life to get twisted by alcoholism is a meaningful personal relationship with Jesus Christ. As a result, these people are ill equipped to discern truth from error when sharing and listening around AA tables.

3. Some believers are unable to put personal biblical beliefs into phrases like "higher power," "Power greater than ourselves," and "God as we understand him."

4. Some meetings are cynical and even anti-Christian. Such meetings usually are dominated by unbelievers who are "sick unto death" with pride. If a person seeking fellowship in AA should encounter one of these groups, AA advises them to find a different group better suited to their needs.

5. Alcoholic Christians need more than AA offers — they need the support of the body of Christ. The Christian alcoholic, though terribly infected, is still a part of the body of Christ.

Have meetings been designed which are specifically Christian in focus?

Yes. There are groups such as the Overcomers, Lion Tamers, Ephesians 5:18, Life Ministries, New Wine, and many others created by local churches and tailored to their faith and practices. These often are called "Aftercare" groups, which refers to the fact that some recovering persons are in a post-treatment phase.

What types of treatments are used in such groups?

Most programs are variations of the Twelve Steps of AA. The Overcomers group in Melbourne, Florida uses the Christian Twelve Steps. These steps are common to Overcomers groups worldwide. (For examples of variations on the AA Twelve Steps, suggested formats for such groups, and possible topics for meetings, see Appendix A.)

Are Christian groups effective?

There are four different views on this. One view is that these groups are the best way for churches to deal with the problems of alcoholism and codependency. Leaders of these groups often relate stories of the healing, growth, and blessings members have experienced.

A second view is that these meetings are ineffective. Some alcoholics and their families have felt, correctly or incorrectly, a spirit of judgmentalism and religious pride. Too often problems are met with simplistic and superficial answers such as, "If a person's faith is strong enough, he will not become alcoholic," or "If you are claiming the promises of the Bible, you have no need to feel trapped, ashamed, guilty, or fearful." Such half-truths, though often expressed with sincerity, cause pain, isolation, and anger. More than a few suffering codependents and alcoholics have turned away from the church. Or the church turns away from them when they, on their way to healing, use the half-truth "AA saved my life."

It takes time, patience, empathy, and Christian love to overcome the thorny problems of broken fellowship. Aftercare groups can become places of reconciliation, but it takes a lot of Christlike conversation and prayer.

The third view of these Christian groups is that they too often, though unintentionally, become intellectual debates on the meaning of Scripture. Members may merely gather Bible information while remaining out of touch with the feeling level of their lives. Intellectualization of doctrine and morals is a common problem in the life of the church, and it offers little or no help in recovery.

Finally, the fourth view is that these groups are just a way for alcoholics and codependents to hide. Those who hold this view believe that Christian alcoholics and codependents must be the salt and light in AA and Al-Anon meetings. Unfortunately, confused Christians caught in addiction and codependency often cannot function as salt and light.

Whatever view one holds of Christian groups, this one fact stands true: the God and Father of our Lord Jesus Christ is the overflowing fountain of *all* good, for everyone, everywhere. Endless discussion about which meetings to attend or create must never keep us from admitting we need help, seeking treatment, working at recovery, and drinking the fresh waters of God's healing love.

FIVE
CHRISTIANS AND RECOVERY

Are alcoholics instantaneously delivered (cured) in religious conversion?

Yes! Thank God, some are healed in this way. Miracles do happen!

It is, however, equally true that many pray daily, sincerely, and trustingly without finding instantaneous deliverance. They are gradually healed in AA, as Christ meets them in the lives of recovering persons, or in treatment centers using the program outlined previously.

God heals in many ways! It is unwise and without Biblical warrant to limit his healing to the moment of religious conversion.

What are some steps a church can take to develop educational programs regarding alcoholism and codependency?

A number of suggested steps in developing a comprehensive response are described below. These can be used as guides for action.

1. Form a planning committee that includes a broad spectrum of interested persons, such as servant-leaders from all existing groups in the church: parents, youth, clergy, seniors, and especially (if possible) recovering members of AA, Al-Anon, or Alateen. Seek out a recovering person who has been in effective

recovery for at least a year and talk with him or her. Ask how that person feels your church could meet the needs of alcoholics or codependents in recovery.

2. Begin with a personal attitude index exercise (see Appendix A). Inform the group that this is not a test, it is only an exercise or an instrument to help discern personal feelings about addictions of all kinds. Follow the exercise with an open discussion. Don't try to settle disagreements, though. Instead, seek to discover specific areas for ministry.

3. Specifically address the biblical, moral, and pastoral issues related to alcoholism, chemical dependency, and codependency. Review existing congregational policies, procedures, programs, and available resources. Some churches have well-developed programs while others have never considered this an appropriate area for church involvement. Many churches are uninformed about available denominational and community resources.

Determine if your denomination or local fellowship of churches has formed a statement regarding these areas. If so, inform the group of the stand taken in the statement.

4. It is important that the group develop a mutual understanding of alcohol use issues to be effective in planning programs. Even so, realize that there often is dissension among believers when it comes to attitudes regarding alcohol use and abuse. Use the questions and answers in this book as a springboard for initial discussion and mutual sharing. But don't wait for *everyone* to agree before you act. Instead, work to reach a majority consensus.

5. Learn what community resources are available to your church. There is specific help available, for free, from deeply caring people in your community whom you never see in your congregation. Thank God that he uses more than just church members to bring healing.

Visit local hospitals and detox units to gain a better understanding of current treatment programs. Talk with local professionals, both Christian and secular, who are trained in the areas of alcoholism and codependency. See if one can direct you to effective educational resources (pamphlets, books, films, etc.), or if any would be willing to lead some workshops or seminars on treatment, recovery, and the Christian's responsibility for those in the congregation who would be interested.

6. Don't try to reinvent the wheel. A marvelous resource for setting into motion specific educational/prevention/intervention programs in your church is The United Presbyterian Church (U.S.A.), the Synod of Lakes and Prairies, 8012 Cedar Ave. S., Bloomington, MN, 55420, 612-854-0144.

Other denominations have specific help available, so contact area clergy. Alcoholism and codependency are nondenominational.

7. Begin now, modestly but decisively. Keep in mind the times God told Moses, and later Joshua (Joshua 7:10), to stop praying and get to work! Appoint small committees to study, formulate written suggestions, and report to the entire group for discussion and adoption. And keep the entire congregation informed of the progress being made.

Why does the phrase "in Christ" hold special meaning for those in recovery?

The Lord's presence *in* us sheds a special light on the paradox alcoholics experience. It is a precious thing for those in recovery to know Christ and to see his presence in their lives. Jesus is known as Immanuel, meaning "God *with* us." He is not far away. But while Jesus dwells *in* and *with* the Christian, he remains beyond him. He is more than and other than the Christian; he is, ever and always, the Lord of lords and King of kings. While he gently, even tenderly, soothes our inner fears, he remains "majestic in holiness" and "working wonders" (Exodus 15:11). He is able to do what needs to be done within the recovering believer to lead him to freedom.

How do Christians often underestimate and restrict Christ's work in recovery?

The confession "I am a sinner" is seldom, if ever, heard as disgusting or degrading. Many church people, however, hear the admission "I am an alcoholic" as repelling and disgusting. This common reaction assumes that Jesus would never use the life of a sick alcoholic to bring another sick person deliverance and healing.

This is a sad assumption. It isolates Christ. It underestimates the surprising ways Jesus works. A powerless alcoholic at an AA meeting reaching out for sobriety finds Christ there. The Lord is present in the life of another alcoholic at the meeting. *Christ lives in alcoholically sick persons as well as in healthy people.* Eyes opened by the Holy Spirit see Jesus *in* hurting people reaching out to heal other hurting people. These are strange ways of healing, but, thank God, his ways are infinitely higher than our ways.

How do freedom, rules, and love relate in a Bible-directed life-style?

1. Jesus Christ makes us free. We need not obey rules of conduct in order to become acceptable (justified or free of blame) to God. Faith in Jesus makes us right with God. Living under grace, we do not bind ourselves with detailed regulations for grateful Christian living. "For the kingdom of God is not a matter of eating and drinking, but of righteousness, peace and joy in the Holy Spirit" (Romans 14:17). Martin Luther caught the spirit of this verse in his *Treatise on Christian Liberty* (1520), when he said, "A Christian is a perfectly free lord of all, subject to none." Only God is Lord of the conscience.

2. Free Christians *may* use alcohol, but there are many reasons not to. It's an undeniable fact: alcohol can produce addiction. Paul, a champion of Christian liberty, said, "All things are lawful for me—but I will not let myself be enslaved by anything" (1 Corinthians 6:12, NAB). Yes, we have freedom, but we must use it with wisdom and discernment. There are many Christians practicing "Christian freedom" who already are in early- and middle-stage alcoholism, and some of these people are not even aware of what is happening to them. Cautious self-examination is always necessary.

3. Freedom is also limited by love of neighbor. Love draws a circle around living freely. Luther spoke of love's limits when he said, "The perfectly free Christian is a perfectly beautiful servant of all." Faith working through love makes us willing

servants of all, and love working through faith makes us lord of all. Through his conduct, a Christian must never knowingly trigger someone else's fall into sin. This is what "being an offense" means. It is not just being an occasion for someone else's dislike or emotional displeasure. An offense, in Bible teaching, is an occasion for another's fall into sin.

It is not a simple matter to set limits. Within local churches there are often differing convictions about love's limits. These differing convictions arise out of painful experiences, dissimilar religious training, and differing ways of reading the Bible. Prayerful study, mutual discussion, and honest sharing must be an ongoing experience as we deal with the teachings of Romans 14, 1 Corinthians 10, Galatians 5, and Colossians 2. Those strong in faith must never condescendingly test the weak in faith. The weak are not to judge the strong. In fact, the Christians who claim to be strong in faith may be weak, and the weak may be stronger than they realize. Mutual respect, sharing, and honesty are needed to find specific limits to love.

4. Christians are called to be examples. In drinking and eating we must display the joyful abandon and the sensitive obedience of Jesus, who changed water to wine to show that his kingdom has come. Living his presence, not merely living *in* his presence, is the key to a life-style of love that sensitively knows where to set limits to avoid being an occasion for someone else to fall into problem drinking.

SIX
AFTERCARE

What are aftercare groups?

Aftercare groups are members of AA, Al-Anon, and Alateen who come together to discuss their faith, growth, and recovery, and to share insights and experiences. Attendance in these groups comes after recovery, when the drug of alcohol is no longer involved. These groups are the greatest need in the Christian community, for they provide a place for those coming out of treatment, where people in recovery can know they will be understood and accepted.

Why are aftercare groups essential for recovery?

Getting sober is hard, but it is harder to *stay* sober. A recovering person needs an environment for growing that is loving, understanding, trusting, but honestly confrontational. He must work on guilt, fear, low self-esteem, and an assortment of other demons.

To avoid relapse, he must continue to learn how to deal with these special problems:

1. *Denial of powerlessness, and a deep need to control.* Christians often have more problems with needing control than others. They expect prayer to be effective, but forget that many prayers aren't prayers at all. Some even delude themselves into thinking they can control grace. They trust growth techniques, forgetting that grace is a pure gift. No one can manipulate God

into giving. He's too wonderful for such games! Flesh wars against grace because it knows no humility.

2. *Shame and guilt*. Secretly, the recovering alcoholic feels inferior to his peers in the pew. Recalling past alcoholic dysfunction, he thinks others are regarding him with disdain, suspicion, and distrust. Although this does happen, recovering persons learn to honestly face these facts, refusing to pout, run, or hide. Sensitive aftercare groups help immensely.

3. *Using alcoholism as an excuse for not taking responsibilities*. The alcoholic did cope with life in many ways, but his alcoholism blunted his ability and exaggerated his problems. Gradually, in aftercare, he learns to assume more and more responsibility, knowing that with the help of Christ and other caring Christians he can recapture responsible and joyful living.

4. *Fear of failure*. While drinking, the alcoholic was afraid of nothing. He felt like a dragon slayer. Not anymore. His chastened mood easily leads to the fear of risk taking. Aftercare group encouragement helps the recovering person to live comfortably with these risks. He learns to reach out again and accept uncertainty. Life is risk! In life there are failures and successes.

5. *Resentments and distrust.* Resentments do not disappear quickly. Trust relationships, difficult to rebuild, can be restored through the power of Christ. But this takes time, honesty, courage, and love, and is especially difficult in fellowships that deny that alcoholism is a disease.

AA's *Big Book* says, "We alcoholics are undisciplined. So we let God discipline us. . . . But this is not all. There is action and more action" (p. 88). Recovery is a lifelong walk, one day at a time, with Jesus. He works his healing miracles through the lives of people in aftercare.

What recovery pitfalls are often discussed in aftercare?

The acronym HALT points to some common pitfalls.

1. *Hungry*. Since alcoholic drinks contain a great deal of sugar, they often are used to calm the pangs of hunger. Do not allow yourself to get too hungry.

2. *Anger*. Be angry, but sin not! Don't let the sun set on your anger.

3. *Loneliness.* Aloneness is fine, but friends are essential.
4. *Tired.* Fatigue cries out for a bracer! Don't get too tired.

What is a peculiar danger for Christians in aftercare sessions?

Both recovering persons and Al-Anon/Alateen persons in aftercare often suffer from a split between conscious intellectual awareness and the unconscious level of ingrained feelings. Intellectually everyone agrees with the following statements:

1. Alcoholism is an illness, not a moral deficiency.
2. The disease is treatable, and can enter remission.
3. All alcoholics are worth treating.
4. The alcoholic is the last person to recognize the illness.
5. Spiritual dimensions are basic for recovery.

This intellectual assent, however, is often made with hidden mental reservations. These reservations produce all kinds of discussions, even heated arguments, about sin, moral responsibility, and sickness. Because these arguments arise out of an unperceived and deeper internal problem, many recovery groups experience tension and needless frustration.

Religious attitudes and convictions are not shaped by intellectual beliefs alone. Traditions in various homes and churches, uncritically accepted, play a strong role in molding fundamental feelings about alcohol issues. Church history shows many strong traditions of moral judgmentalism dismissing alcoholics as morally weak and careless, effectively banning them from religious fellowship, even turning them over to "demon-rum." Jokes about the church drunk are common. These traditions and attitudes are stored at subconscious levels of selfhood and block the intellectually correct beliefs mentioned above from functioning effectively. Both helpers and those being helped alike are victimized by this unperceived split between conscious convictions and subconscious attitudes. Misunderstanding compounds when people *argue alongside* one another, rather than *dialogue with* one another.

To help promote enlightened discussions in aftercare, we previously answered some biblically oriented questions. Church members with a heart for Christian ministry in aftercare may wish to use these, perhaps discovering more questions and better answers as they walk this path of love.

What is a pre-condition for helping others in recovery?

One must be comfortable with his own attitudes and actions concerning drinking. Beware of "Bible-based" rationalizations. "All gifts may be used with thanksgiving by free Christians. No one can tell me it's wrong to drink! Why cramp my style just because others can't drink moderately?"

Romans 14:17 can be used as an excuse for ignoring an alcohol-related problem: "The kingdom of God is not a matter of eating and drinking, but of righteousness, peace and joy in the Holy Spirit."

No one wants to curtail freedom in Christ. Remember, however, that alcohol is a drug. It has addicted tens of thousands of people. Could you possibly be an early-stage alcoholic? How important is your daily beer or cocktail? Can you be just as happy without it? How much *real* difference does a drink make for you? Is it boss in your life?

"Bible text" rationalizations are still rationalizations. They may be the fuel of denial, the greatest symptom of alcoholism. Begin with honest self-appraisal.

What short formula can be used for self-appraisal?

To get started, honestly use the CAGE questionnaire:

C: Have you ever thought you ought to *cut down* on drinking?

A: Have people ever *annoyed* you by criticizing your drinking?

G: Have you ever felt bad or *guilty* about your drinking?

E: Have you ever had a drink first thing in the morning (an *"eye-opener"*) to steady your nerves or get rid of a hangover?

If you have answered yes to any of these questions, you should consider talking with a professional counselor to determine if you have a problem.

APPENDIX A:
CHRISTIAN RECOVERY GROUPS

SUGGESTED FORMAT AND TOPICS

Format

You may use this suggested format as it is, or modify it to fit your particular group and its needs.

1. Designated leader opens the group, *on time,* with a greeting: "Hi, everyone. My name is _____ , and this is the regular meeting of (group name)."

2. Leader gives an opening prayer.

3. Ask if there are any first-time visitors. Welcome them and have them give their first names only, then have everyone introduce themselves by first name.

4. If leader wishes, pass out song sheets and have group sing several songs to warm up.

5. Ask someone to read the group's Preamble:

> _____*(Name of group)*_____ *is a fellowship of men and women who have been affected either directly or indirectly by the abuse of alcohol and/or mood-altering chemicals. We believe that as we look to a loving God for help, and put into practice those principles for living that he has given in his word, the Bible, we shall find both the strength and freedom we need to live productive and happy lives.*
>
> *We strongly believe that our higher power is Jesus Christ, our Savior and Lord. Our primary purpose, based directly upon the word of God, is as follows: (1) To provide fellowship in recovery, (2) To be and to live reconciled to God and his family, (3) To gain a better understanding of alcohol and mood-altering chemicals and addiction, (4) To be built up and strengthened in our faith in Christ, and (5) To render dedicated service to others who are suffering as we once suffered.*
>
> *We hold no corporate opinions concerning politics, economics, race, philosophy, science, or any other matter not immediately bearing upon our recovery. While we do believe that Jesus is the Christ, the resurrected and living Son of God, we hold no corporate view concerning denominational preference.*
>
> *We practice the suggested Twelve Step recovery program of Alcoholics Anonymous and Al-Anon because we believe these to be principles that are clearly set forth in Scripture.*
>
> *We welcome anyone who has a desire to stay clean and sober; anyone who has a desire to rise above the pain and turmoil resulting from*

the addiction of self or of a loved one; anyone who is not opposed to our general method of recovery. We are here to share our experience, strength, and hope with one another. The loving support and genuine caring of fellow members, coupled with daily prayer and the reading of Scripture, prepares us to experience total serenity in Christ, no matter what our outward circumstances might be. Attendance at additional Twelve Step groups is encouraged.

We are zealously dedicated to the principles of anonymity and confidentiality. Nothing said in these discussions will leave this room in any form. Gossip has no place among us, nor will we share these discussions with outside prayer lists.

Our common welfare must come first. Our leaders are chosen not to govern, but to serve. There is only one authority in our group: Jesus Christ, as he expresses his love among us.

6. Ask someone to read the Twelve Steps (see following section of Appendix A or page 91), followed by the group saying the Serenity Prayer in unison: "God grant me the serenity to accept the things I cannot change, the courage to change the things I can, and the wisdom to know the difference."

7. Topical Study Time. Choose a topic from the Suggested Topics list (see next section of Appendix A) or from other program-related material. The leader should assign Scripture passages, Al-Anon pages, AA Big Book pages, etc., to those in the group who wish to participate. As individuals read the specific material, they are given opportunity to make comments on what they have read. Limit this portion of the meeting to approximately 30 minutes.

8. Sharing Time. The leader should go around the room and ask each person to share his or her feelings and related experiences of the day or week. Everyone has the right to "pass," no one should feel pressured to participate. The leader should be sensitive and alert to any special problems that need to be addressed, and avoid any disruptions or attempts to dominate the discussion. Try to make certain that everyone who wishes to share has an opportunity to do so. Limit this portion of the meeting to approximately one hour.

9. Prayer Time. Ask for prayer requests regarding either the attendees themselves or other group members. Designate someone to begin sentence prayers. Either another designated person or the leader should close. The Lord's Prayer can be used to close.

Suggested Topics for Meetings
How habits are formed
Dos and don'ts for the family members
Denial defined
Intervention
Alcoholism and the family
Drug abuse and addiction
Perils of prescription drugs
Dealing with depression, guilt, and self-pity
The overcoming life-style
Detachment

Your personal rehabilitation contract
The road to recovery
Why people drink (or use drugs)
The Serenity Prayer

Topics with Suggested Scriptures

Actions: Walk like you talk — Isa. 30:21; Rom. 6:4; 1 Cor. 4:20; 2 Cor. 5:7; Gal. 5:16; Eph. 4:1; 5:2,15

Dealing with Anger/Resentment — Psa. 37:8-11; Prov. 14:17; 15:1; 16:32; 19:11; 20:22; 22:24; Eccles. 7:9; Matt. 5:21-26,39; James 1:19-20; 1 Pet. 3:8-18)

Blame/Excuses — Gen. 3:9-15; Exod. 32:19-24; 1 Sam. 13:11-14; 15:16-23; Jer. 1:6-7; Luke 14:15-24; Rom. 1:20

Courage — Deut 31:1-6; 2 Chron. 32:1-8; Psa. 27:14; 28:6-9; 46:1-2; 91; 118:5-7; 143:5-10; John 16:33; Eph. 6:10-17; Phil. 1:27-28

Dependence upon God — Deut. 33:27; 2 Chron. 20:6-12; Psa. 127:1; 139:1-5; Jer. 10:23-24; Matt. 28:18; John 3:22-27; 15:5; 2 Cor. 3:4-5

Freedom — Gen. 2:16; Matt. 10:8; John 8:32; Rom. 6:7,22; 8:2,21; Gal. 5:1,13-14; 1 Pet. 2:16

Friendship with God — Exod. 33:11; Job 16:20-22; Psa. 38:11; 149:4-5; 147:1-11; Prov. 17:17; 18:24; Matt. 11:19; 28:20; John 15:13-14; Acts 17:28-29; Heb. 13:5-6; James 4:4-10

God's Will — Psa. 40:6-8; 143:5-10; Matt. 12:46-50; 26:42; John 17:14-19; Rom. 12:1-2; Eph. 6:6-7; James 4:13-16

Gratitude — Psa. 9:11-12; 106:1; 107:1-2; Isa. 12:1-2; Matt. 15:21-31; Luke 15:11-32; 17:11-19; 2 Cor. 4:15-18; Col. 1:12-14; Heb. 13:11-16; 1 Pet. 2:7-10

Honesty — Lev. 19:11,35-36; Prov. 16:8; Rom. 12:17; 13:12-14; 2 Cor. 8:16-21; 13:7; Phil. 4:8; 1 Pet. 3:10; 1 John 1:8-9

Let Go and Let God (Powerlessness, Surrender) — Psa. 31:24; 33:18-22; 39:1-7; 42:9-11; 46:1; 71:1-5; Jer. 17:7-8; 2 Cor. 1:9

Live and Let Live (Acceptance, Criticism, Judging) — Matt. 7:1,3-5; Luke 10:38-42; Rom. 2:1; 14:4,13; 1 Cor. 4:5; 1 Thess. 4:11

One Day at a Time (Anxiety, Fear, Worry, Faith) — Deut. 28:67; Matt. 6:25-34; Luke 12:11-12,25-26; Phil. 4:6; 1 Pet. 5:7

Open-mindedness — Prov. 18:15; Isa. 30:21; 32:18-19; 55:8-9; Hosea. 12:6; Matt. 8:3; 16:23; 21:31; Mark 9:23; 12:10-11; Luke 23:43; John 9:39; 2 Cor. 10:3; Eph. 3:16,20; Heb. 3:10

Overcoming — Psa. 40:1-2; Isa. 40:28-31; Nahum 1:7; John 1:16-17; 8:31-32; 16:33; Rom. 12:21; 13:14; Gal. 4:8-9; 5:13-16; 2 Tim. 4:14-17; 1 John 5:4-5

Serenity (Peace) — Psa. 5:11; 16:11; 30:5; 51:12; 146:5; Prov. 17:22; Isa. 26:3; Jer. 15:16; Matt. 5:6-10; John 15:11; Phil. 4:6-7; 1 Pet. 1:8; 3:11

Vengeance — Lev. 19:18; Prov. 20:22; 24:28-29; Matt. 5:38-39; Rom. 12:14-18; 1 Pet. 3:9

Willingness — Exod. 35:5; Judg. 5:1-2; 8:23-25; Neh. 11:1-2; Psa. 110:3; Isa. 1:18-19; 2 Cor. 8:1-3; 1 Thess. 2:8

VARIATIONS ON AA'S TWELVE STEPS

Rewritten Twelve Steps

1. We admitted that we were powerless over alcohol or the alcoholic (the substance we had abused or the substance abuser) and that our lives had become unmanageable.

"There is a way that seems right to a man, but in the end it leads to death" (Prov. 14:12).

"For what I do is not the good I want to do; no, the evil I do not want to do—this I keep on doing" (Rom. 7:19).

"What a wretched man I am! Who will rescue me from this body of death?" (Rom. 7:24).

Other Scripture: Gen. 4:7; Prov. 3:5-8; 14:12; John 8:34-36; Rom. 3:10,23; 6:23; 7:5-6,18-20,24-25; 8:1-2,9-10; 1 Cor. 10:13-14; 2 Cor. 1:9; 1 Pet. 5:6-7.

2. We came to believe that through Jesus Christ we could be restored to a right relationship with God the Father, and to subsequent sanity and stability in our lives.

"Jesus answered, 'I am the way and the truth and the life. No one comes to the Father except through me'" (John 14:6).

"For my Father's will is that everyone who looks to the Son and believes in him shall have eternal life" (John 6:40).

"Everyone who calls on the name of the Lord will be saved" (Rom. 10:13).

Other Scripture: Isa. 1:18-20; John 3:3-5; 6:37-40; 7:37-39; 10:37-39; 11:25-26; 14:1-4; 17:15-26; 20:29-31; Rom. 8:11; 10:1-4,13; 2 Cor. 4:13-14; Rev. 3:20.

3. We made a decision to turn from things of the past and invite Jesus Christ to be Lord and manager of our lives.

"That if you confess with your mouth, 'Jesus is Lord,' and believe in your heart that God raised him from the dead, you will be saved. For it is with your heart that you believe and are justified, and it is with your mouth that you confess and are saved" (Rom. 10:9-10).

Other Scripture: Prov. 16:3; Matt. 11:28-30; John 3:16-18,36; 10:17-18; 12:24; Rom. 5:17; 6:12-14; 10:9-10; 1 Cor. 15:22; 2 Cor. 5:15-21; 6:2; Phil. 1:13-16; 1 John 4:15-17.

4. We made a searching and fearless moral inventory of ourselves.

"Have nothing to do with the fruitless deeds of darkness, but rather expose them" (Eph. 5:11).

"Godly sorrow brings repentance that leads to salvation and leaves no regret, but worldly sorrow brings death" (2 Cor. 7:10).

Other Scripture: Psa. 19:14; 139:23-24; Ezek. 36:26-27,31; Mark 7:20-23; John 8:34-36; Rom. 8:5-9; 12:1-3; 13:11-14; 2 Cor. 6:14–7:1; 7:10; Gal. 5:13-16; Eph. 4:17–5:21; 1 John 1:8; 3:19-24.

5. We admitted to Jesus Christ, ourselves, and another human being the exact nature of our wrongs.

"If we claim to be without sin, we deceive ourselves and the truth is not in us. If we confess our sins, he is faithful and just and will forgive us our sins and purify us from all unrighteousness" (1 John 1:8-9).

"Therefore confess your sins to each other and pray for each other so that you may be healed" (James 5:16a).

"The night is nearly over; the day is almost here. So let us put aside the deeds of darkness and put on the armor of light" (Rom. 13:12).

Other Scripture: Psa. 32:1-5; Prov. 20:9; 28:13; Luke 12:2-3; John 3:19-21; 1 John 1:8-10; 2:1-2; James 5:16.

6. We were entirely ready to have God through Jesus Christ remove all of our character defects.

"No one who is born of God will continue to sin, because God's seed remains in him; he cannot go on sinning, because he has been born of God" (1 John 3:9).

"Therefore, I urge you, brothers, in view of God's mercy, to offer your bodies as living sacrifices, holy and pleasing to God — this is your spiritual act of worship" (Rom. 12:1).

Other Scripture: John 1:29; Acts 3:19; Rom. 12:1-2; Gal. 1:3-5; Eph. 1:17; 2:3-5; 4:31-32; 2 Tim. 2:15; Heb. 4:13-16; 8:10-12; 1 Pet. 5:6-7; 1 John 3:4-6,9-10.

7. We humbly asked Jesus Christ to remove our shortcomings — believing he would remove them — and to forgive us.

"He who conceals his sins does not prosper, but whoever confesses and renounces them finds mercy" (Prov. 28:13).

"Then I acknowledged my sin to you and did not cover up my iniquity. I said, 'I will confess my transgressions to the Lord' — and you forgave the guilt of my sin" (Psa. 32:5).

"Create in me a pure heart, O God, and renew a steadfast spirit within me" (Psa. 51:10).

Other Scripture: Psa. 32:5; 41:4; 51:1-13; Prov. 1:7; 15:33; 20:9; 22:4; 28:13; Matt. 3:1-2; 18:1-4; Luke 18:10-14; Heb. 11:6; 1 Pet. 5:6-7; 1 John 1:9.

8. We made a list of all people we had harmed, and became willing to make amends to them all.

"Fools mock at making amends for sin, but goodwill is found among the upright" (Prov. 14:9).

"Therefore, if you are offering your gift at the altar and there remember that your brother has something against you, leave your gift there in front of the altar. First go and be reconciled to your brother; then come and offer your gift" (Matt. 5:23-24).

Other Scripture: Prov. 14:9; 20:22; 24:29; Matt. 5:21-24; 6:14-15; 7:12; Mark 11:25; Luke 6:27-29; John 13:34-35; 1 Pet. 4:7-8; 1 John 2:9-11.

9. We made direct amends to such people whenever possible, except when to do so would injure them or others.

"Give everyone what you owe him: If you owe taxes, pay taxes; if revenue, then revenue; if respect, then respect; if honor, then honor. Let no debt remain outstanding, except the continuing debt to love one another, for he who loves his fellowman has fulfilled the law" (Rom. 13:7-8).

"Who is going to harm you if you are eager to do good?" (1 Pet. 3:13).

Other Scripture: Prov. 25:21-22; Ezek. 33:14-15; Matt. 25:40; Rom. 13:7-8; 1 Pet. 3:13.

10. We continued to take personal inventory, and when we were wrong we promptly admitted it.

"For by the grace given me I say to every one of you: Do not think of yourself more highly than you ought, but rather think of yourself with sober judgment, in accordance with the measure of faith God has given you" (Rom. 12:3).

"Do nothing out of selfish ambition or vain conceit, but in humility consider others better than yourselves" (Phil. 2:3).

Other Scripture: Luke 12:1-3; Rom. 12:3; 1 Cor. 10:12-13; 13:4-7,11; Eph. 4:25; Phil. 2:1-4; 2 Tim. 2:23-24; Heb. 9:13-14; James 1:22; 1 Pet. 1:22-23; 2:16-17; 1 John 1:9; 2:1-2.

11. We sought through prayer and meditation on God's word to increase our fellowship with him, praying continually for the knowledge of his will for us and the power of his might to accomplish it.

"My son, pay attention to what I say; listen closely to my words. Do not let them out of your sight, keep them within your heart; for they are life to those who find them and health to a man's whole body" (Prov. 4:20-22).

"Ask and it will be given to you; seek and you will find; knock and the door will be opened to you. For everyone who asks receives; he who seeks finds; and to him who knocks, the door will be opened" (Matt. 7:7-8).

"Be joyful always; pray continually; give thanks in all circumstances, for this is God's will for you in Christ Jesus" (1 Thess. 5:16-18).

Other Scripture: Psa. 1:1-3; 19:14; 40:8; 119:10-11; 143:10; Matt. 6:5-13; 7:7-8; 12:50; 18:18-20; 26:41; John 16:23-24; Acts 1:14; 4:29-31; 2 Cor. 10:4-5; Eph. 3:14-19; 6:18; 1 Thess. 5:16-18.

12. Having been spiritually restored and set free from the 'sin which does so easily beset us,' we attempt to share this freedom, and the One who has brought it to us, with those who still suffer, we work to practice the Lord's principles in all our affairs.

"You will receive power when the Holy Spirit comes on you; and you will be my witnesses in Jerusalem, and in all Judea and Samaria, and to the ends of the earth" (Acts 1:8).

"Brothers, if someone is caught in a sin, you who are spiritual should restore him gently. But watch yourself, or you may also be tempted" (Gal. 6:1).

"The end of all things is near. Therefore be clear minded and self-controlled so that you can pray. Above all, love each other deeply, because love covers over a multitude of sins" (1 Pet. 4:7-8).

Other Scripture: Matt. 9:35-38; 10:7-8; 16:33; John 8:31-32; 15:7-8, 15-17; Rom. 10:14-17; 1 Cor. 9:19-23; 2 Cor. 1:3-4; Gal. 6:1-2; 2 Tim. 4:3-5; 1 Pet. 5:8-9; Jude 20:23

Unaltered AA Twelve Steps expanded with Scripture

1. We admitted that we were powerless over alcohol — that our lives had become unmanageable.
   A. Powerlessness and helplessness — Num. 11:14-17; Jer. 9:23-24; Luke 13:10-13; John 15:5; Rom. 5:1-6; 7:18–8:2; 2 Cor. 1:9; 3:4-5.
   B. Man's weakness becomes God's opportunity to help — Psa. 116:5-9; Mark 4:35-41; 5:21-29.
   C. Strength in weakness — 2 Cor. 12:1-10; Heb. 11:32-34.

2. We came to believe that a power greater than ourselves could restore us to sanity.
   A. Examples of weak faith — Matt. 6:28-30; 8:23-26; 14:23-32.
   B. Examples of strong faith — Matt. 8:1-3,23-26; 9:18-25,27-29.
   C. Obstacles that test faith of believers — Matt. 15:21-28; Mark 5:35-36; 10:13; Luke 5:17-26; John 9:1-25; 11:1-6.
   D. Insanity — Psa. 14:1; Prov. 12:15.

3. We made a decision to turn our will and our lives over to the care of God, as we understood him.
   A. The surrendered life — Matt. 11:28-30; John 10:1-10; Gal. 2:20.
   B. Submission to Divine will — Psa. 32:8-9; 40; 143:10-11; Prov. 3:5-6; 28:26.
   C. Pleasing God — Prov. 16:7.
   D. Understanding — Psa. 119:104-106; Prov. 2:6.
   E. Salvation through Christ — John 3:16; Acts 2:21; 4:12; 15:11.

4. We made a searching and fearless moral inventory of ourselves.
   A. Principle of cataloging — Deut. 30:1-3; Psa. 32:3-5; 51:3; Prov. 28:13; Isa. 59:9-12; Jer. 3:13; 14:20-22; Lam. 3:20-23,39-40; 1 John 1:5-10.
   B. Inventory of ourselves — Matt. 7:1-5; Eph. 4:31-32; 2 Pet. 1:5-10.
   C. Willingness to forgive others — Matt. 6:14-15; Eph. 4:31-32; Col. 3:12-13.

5. We admitted to God, to ourselves, and to another human being the exact nature of our wrongs.
   A. Principle of confession — Psa. 32:3-5; Prov. 28:13; Gal. 6:13; James 5:16.
   B. Examples of confession — 1 Sam. 15:24; 2 Sam. 12:13; Matt. 3:1-6; Luke 15:11-32; Acts 19:13-20.
   C. Need for honesty — Rom. 12:17; 2 Cor. 8:16-21; 1 Pet. 2:12.

6. We were entirely ready to have God remove all these defects of character.
   A. Humility/Acknowledging defects — Heb. 12:1-2.
   B. Being ready for pruning of self-will — 2 Tim. 2:20-22.
   C. Preparation precedes blessings — 2 Kings 3:16-20; 4:1-7; Hosea 10:12; Joel 2:12-13.

D. Principle of cleansing—Psa. 103:10-12; Isa. 1:18; Micah 7:18-20; Rom. 6:1-14; 2 Cor. 5:15-17; 1 John 1:9.

7. We humbly asked him to remove our shortcomings.
   A. Humility—Prov. 16:18-19; 22:4; 29:23; Isa. 57:15; Micah 6:8; James 4:7-10.
   B. Examples of humility—Gen. 32:9-10; 1 Sam. 9:15-21; 2 Sam. 17:1-18; 1 Kings 3:3-7.
   C. Promises to the humble—Isa. 66:1-2; Matt. 5:1-3; Luke 14:7-11; 2 Cor. 8:9; 12:7-10.

8. We made a list of all persons we had harmed, and became willing to make amends to them all.
   A. Preparation precedes blessings—Matt. 5:23-24.
   B. Willingness—Neh. 11:1-2; Isa. 1:18-19; 2 Cor. 8:3,9-12; 1 Pet. 5:2.

9. We made direct amends to such people whenever possible, except when to do so would injure them or others.
   A. Get rid of the weight—Heb. 12:1.
   B. Reconciliation with a brother—Matt. 18:15.
   C. Reconciliation with God through Christ—2 Cor. 5:18-21; Eph. 2:14-18; Col. 1:20; Heb. 2:17-18.

10. We continued to take personal inventory, and when we were wrong, promptly admitted it.
   A. Principles of continuance—Psa. 139:23-24; Rom. 6:1-4; Gal. 6:1-5; 2 Tim. 3:14.
   B. Confession—Matt. 5:43-44; 6:12; Eph. 4:23-32; James 5:16; 1 John 1:8-10.
   C. Letting God examine you when you question a wrong—Psa. 26:1-12; Prov. 28:13-14; Lam. 3:39-40.

11. We sought through prayer and meditation to improve our conscious contact with God, as we understood him, praying only for knowledge of his will for us and the power to carry that out.
   A. Prayer—Matt. 6:5-15; Luke 11:1-13; 18:1-8; John 17.
   B. Holy Spirit aids in prayer—1 Chron. 16:11; Matt. 7:7-11; 26:39-41; James 5:13.
   C. Prayer answered—Exod. 15:25; Judg. 6:36-40; 1 Kings 18:36-39.
   D. Promises of answer—Isa. 65:24; John 15:5-7.
   E. Causes of failure—Psa. 66:16-20; 2 Cor. 12:8-10.
   F. Meditation—Psa. 1:2; 19:12-14.

12. Having had a spiritual awakening as a result of these steps, we tried to carry this message to alcoholics and to practice these principles in all our affairs.
   A. Spiritual awakening is essential—Matt. 18:1-3.
   B. Carry the message—Isa. 52:7; Matt. 10:8; John 4:34-38; Rom. 10:14-15; 1 Pet. 3:15.

PERSONAL ATTITUDE INDEX

	Agree	Disagree	Uncertain
1. *Drunkenness and alcoholism are the same thing.*	A	D	U
2. *Alcoholics and heroin addicts have entirely different problems.*	A	D	U
3. *Chemically dependent people have basic personality flaws.*	A	D	U
4. *To truly love someone who is chemically dependent, you must accept him as he is.*	A	D	U
5. *The whole family is part of a chemical dependency problem.*	A	D	U
6. *Chemically dependent people can really be helped only if they are "down and out."*	A	D	U
7. *Chemically dependent people suffer from a disease over which they have no willful control.*	A	D	U
8. *Most chemically dependent people would never forgive a spouse for forcing them into treatment.*	A	D	U
9. *An alcoholic is as blameless for his condition as a diabetic is for his condition.*	A	D	U
10. *More than one out of ten of all alcoholics are on skid row.*	A	D	U
11. *Virtually anyone who consumes a large enough quantity of alcohol over a long enough period of time will develop alcoholism.*	A	D	U
12. *A person who consumes nothing stronger than beer is probably not an alcoholic.*	A	D	U
13. *One may be a good worker on the job and still be chemically depen-. dent*	A	D	U
14. *One can get just as addicted to tranquilizers as to alcohol.*	A	D	U
15. *People who are chemically depen- dent generally lack strength of character.*	A	D	U

APPENDIX B:
RESOURCES

BOOKS

Anonymous
Alcoholics Anonymous. New York, N.Y.: AA World Services, Inc., 1976.
Alcoholics Anonymous Comes to Age. New York, N.Y.: AA World Services, Inc., 1975.
Alateen: Hope for Children of Alcoholics. New York, N.Y.: Al-Anon Family Group Headquarters, Inc., 1985.
Al-Anon Faces Alcoholism. New York, N.Y.: Al-Anon Family Group Headquarters, Inc., 1984.
Came to Believe. New York, N.Y.: Alcoholics Anonymous World Services, Inc., 1982.
Twelve Steps and Twelve Traditions. New York, N.Y.: AA World Services, Inc., 1982.
Bass, Ellen & Davis, Laura. *The Courage to Heal.* New York, N.Y.: Harper and Row, 1988.
Beattie, Melody. *Codependent No More.* New York, N.Y.: Harper and Row, 1987.
Black, Claudia. *Children of Alcoholics.* New York, N.Y.: Ballantine Books, 1981.
Bradshaw, John. *Health Communications.* Pompano Beach, FL.: 1988.
DeJong, Alexander C. *Help and Hope for the Alcoholic.* Wheaton: Tyndale House, 1986.
Drews, T. *Getting Them Sober (Vols. 1 & 2).* Plainfield, N.J.: Bridge Publishing, 1980, 1983.
Goodwin, D. *Is Alcoholism Hereditary?* New York, N.Y.: Oxford University Press, 1976.
Jellinek, E. M. *The Disease Concept of Alcoholism.* New Haven, CT: College and University Press, 1960.
Johnson, Vernon. *I'll Quit Tomorrow.* New York, N.Y.: Harper & Row, 1980.
Keller, John. *Ministering to Alcoholics.* Minneapolis: Augsburg, 1966.
Kellerman, J. *Alcoholism: A Merry-Go-Round Named Denial.* Center City, MN: Augsburg Publishing House, 1966.
Mann, Marty. *New Primer on Alcoholism.* New York, N.Y.: Holt, Rhinehart, and Winston, 1981.
Martin, Greg. *Spiritus Contra Spiritum.* Philadelphia: Westminster Press, 1977.
Milan, J. and Ketcham, L. *Under the Influence.* New York, N.Y.: Bantam Books, 1983.
Ohlms, D., *The Disease Concept of Alcoholism.* Belleville, IL: Gary Whiteaker Company, 1983.

Stein, R. "Wine, Drinking in the New Testament Times." *Christianity Today,* (June 20, 1979): 9-11.

Spickard, A., MD, and B. Thompson. *Dying for a Drink.* Waco: Word Books, 1985.

Subby, Robert. *Lost in the Shuffle.* Pompano Beach, FL: Health Communications, 1987.

Timmer, John. *God of Weakness.* Grand Rapids, MI: Zondervan, 1985.

Thompson, Barbara. "Alcoholism: Even the Church is Hurting." *Christianity Today,* (August, 1983): 24-28.

Wegscheider, Sharon. *Another Chance.* Palo Alto, CA: Science and Behavior Publication, 1981.

Wholey, D., *The Courage to Change.* Boston, MA: Houghton Mifflin Company, 1984.

Woititz, J. *Adult Children of Alcoholics.* Pompano Beach, FL: Health Communications, 1983.

Woititz, J. *Struggle for Intimacy.* Pompano Beach, FL: Health Communications, 1985.

FILMS

Al-Anon Speaks for Itself. New York: N.Y.: Al-Anon Family Group Headquarters, 1986.

Disease Concept of Alcoholism and Disease Concept of Alcoholism II (featuring David Ohlms). Belleville, IL: Gary Whiteaker Company, Inc.

The Enablers. Minneapolis, MN: The Johnson Institute

The Intervention. Minneapolis, MN: The Johnson Institute.

The Disease Concept of Alcoholism. Ohlms.

The Family Trap. Sharon Wegscheider.

Soft is the Heart of a Child. San Diego, CA: Operation Cork.

Other sources of film and videos

   Hazelden Educational Services

   Box 176

   Center City, MN 55012

   1-800-328-9288

   Also contact local treatment centers, hospitals, and chapters of AA, Al-Anon, and Alateen for list of films and videos.

NATIONAL ORGANIZATIONS

(For local meetings refer to yellow pages of the local phone book.)

Al-Anon Family Group
P.O. Box 182, Madison Square Garden
New York, NY 10159
(212) 481-6565

Alcohol and Drug Problems Association of North America (ADPA)
1101 15th Street, NW
Washington, DC 20005
(202) 452-0990

Alcoholics Anonymous
General Service Office
468 Park Avenue South
New York, NY 10016
(212) 686-1100

Narc-Anon Family Group
P.O. Box 2562
Palos Verdes, CA 90274
(213) 547-5800

Narcotics Anonymous
World Service Office
P.O. Box 622
Sun Valley, CA 91325
(213) 768-6203

National Alcoholism Treatment Directory ($5.00)
Alcoholism/The National Magazine
Box C 19051
Seattle, WA 98109
(800) 528-6600, ext. 100

National Association of Alcoholism Counselors
951 S. George Mason Drive
Arlington, VA 22204
(703) 920-8338

National Association of Alcoholism Treatment Programs
2082 Mickelson Dr., Suite 200
Irvine, CA 92715
(714) 975-0104

National Black Alcoholism Council
100 Maryland Avenue, NE
Washington, DC 20005

National Clearinghouse for Alcohol Information
Box 2345
Rockville, MD 20852
(301) 468-2600

National Clearinghouse for Drug Abuse Information
P.O. Box 722
Kensington, MD 20901

National Coalition of Hispanic Mental Health and Human Services Organizations
1010 15th Street, NW, Suite 402
Washington, DC 20005

National Council on Alcoholism (NCA)
733 Third Avenue
New York, NY 10017
(212) 986-4433

National Episcopal Coalition on Alcohol
P.O. Box 50489
Washington, DC 20004

National Federation of Parents for Drug-Free Youth
P.O. Box 722
Silver Springs, MD 20901
(301) 593-9256

National Indian Board on Alcohol and Drug Abuse
P.O. Box 8
Turtle Lake, WI 54889

National Institute on Drug Abuse (NIDA)
5600 Fishers Lane
Rockville, MD 20857

National PTA–Alcohol/Drug Education Project
700 North Rush Street
Chicago, IL 60611
(312) 787-0977

North Conway Institute
14 Beacon Street
Boston, MA 02108
(617) 742-0424

Parkside Medical Services Corporation
Martin Doot, Director
205 W. Touhy Ave.
Park Ridge, IL 60068
(708) 692-9660

Prevention of Alcohol Problems, Inc.
4616 Longfellow Avenue S
Minneapolis, MN 55407
(612) 729-3047

Pride
100 Edgewood Avenue, Suite 1216
Atlanta, GA 30303
(800) 282-4241

INDEX